# Mastering the Art of Wok Cooking

with step-by-step instructions

# Mastering the Art of Wok Cooking

with step-by-step instructions

## Jacki Passmore

Photographer Ray Joyce

**WeLDoN** PUBLISHING
SYDNEY · LONDON

The Publishers would like to thank the following for
their kind assistance in lending us props for photography:

Quality Café and Club Equipment, Sydney
Thebe International, Sydney
Mikasa Tableware, Sydney
KWL's Import Pty Ltd, Sydney
Finnish Importing, Sydney
Asia Provisions Pty Ltd, Chatswood N.S.W.

Food styled by June Budgen

A Kevin Weldon Production

Published by Weldon Publishing
a division of Kevin Weldon & Associates Pty Limited
Sydney, Australia

First published by Lansdowne Press 1986
Reprinted by Weldon Publishing 1992

© Copyright: Kevin Weldon & Associates Pty Limited
© Copyright design: Kevin Weldon & Associates Pty Limited

Managing editor: Susan Tomnay
Editor: Beverley Barnes
Designer: Sarah Laffey

Typeset in Australia by Savage Type, Brisbane, in Plantin
Printed in Singapore by Kyodo Printing Co. (S'pore) Pte Ltd

National Library of Australia Cataloguing-in-Publication data

Passmore, Jacki.
    Mastering the art of wok cooking, with step-by-step instructions.

    Includes index.
    ISBN 1 86302 186 8.

    1. Wok cookery. I. Joyce, Ray, 1947-   . II. Title.

641.589

# Contents

# Introduction

Might it have occurred to a Sung Dynasty housewife sometime between A.D. 960 and 1126 in northern China that a cooking vessel identical to her own *wok* would be in active use 900 years later? Then it was used as a multi-functional cooking pan, and today it remains the only pan ideally suited to stir-frying, as well as serving as domestic deep-fryer, steamer, poacher, frying pan and stewpan—not to mention smoker, campfire saucepan and table-top flambé or fondue pot.

I have a particular fondness for wok cooking, having lived and cooked in the Far East for ten years. My kitchen, like the majority of kitchens in Hong Kong's multi-storey buildings, was cramped and basic. It comprised a tiled bench on which sat a two-burner gas cooker, and a deep porcelain sink. There was just room to squeeze in a refrigerator, but no cupboards for pots and pans and cooking equipment, much less food provisions.

A rack and a series of hooks on the wall behind the cooker solved the problem of storage for my cooking utensils, and they were always easy to find and handy to the cooking area. A few shelves were put up, and I found myself equipped for full-scale Chinese cooking.

I studied and cooked Chinese food with a passion for weeks, months, but then my husband developed the expatriate 'blues'. Could I accomplish something English in my wok? The resultant steamed Steak and Kidney Pudding he had to admit quite equalled his mum's.

Heartened that I wasn't going to be completely limited to Chinese cooking, I began a spate of International dishes. Cooking in the wok had become an intellectual challenge as well as a physical one. From then on curries, casseroles, puddings, desserts and vegetable dishes of all description and origin began to emerge—many with outstanding success, some that needed modifications, but on the whole there were very few disasters.

Thank goodness for notebooks and a good filing system, for years later when Lansdowne asked me to put together this book, I knew immediately what would go into it. So in many ways this has been something of a nostalgic exercise for me, as well as providing my family and friends with many weeks of delightful dinners.

Woks are now in use in domestic kitchens and many restaurants around the world. The wok is a unique and very practical type of pan. It's inexpensive, wears well, cleans easily, rarely burns or buckles if overheated and requires no special between-use care save a light coating of cooking oil to prevent rusting.

The traditional wok is made of pressed or rolled steel. It may not score highly for aesthetics, but once it has acquired its 'seasoning' it will never let you down. Wok manufacturers nowadays, however, have become quite fanciful in the designing of woks for today's use.

A variety of sizes and depths has always been necessary in the range of woks sold to Chinese cooks, but now we can also choose from Teflon-lined aluminium woks, tinned copper woks, stainless steel woks, stone-finish cast-iron woks, and so on. There are woks with the traditional curved bottom and woks with flat bases for use on electric hotplates; there are woks with one long handle, woks with pouring lips and woks finished with a selection of 'designer' colours.

And there are electric woks: thin aluminium woks which accompany a small portable electric ring; plug-in-type electric woks which work on the principle of the 'frypan'; and electric skillet-type woks of sturdy cast iron. Portable cookers too have developed alongside the creation of this vast range of woks. One-burner gas rings, table-top electric cookers, even wok-holes in barbecue cookers for outdoor wok cooking are now available.

For most dishes I remain faithful to my gas wok-cooker and the traditional pressed-steel wok, but frequently use also a flat-bottomed wok on my electric cooker, and my electric wok which I manage to retrieve from my mother every now and then.

The sort of wok you ultimately choose will be dictated by several factors: your cooking source, anticipated frequency of use and budget. Unlike the purchasing of saucepans, though, the most expensive wok may not necessarily be the best suited to your purpose. Having tested a one-handled wok lately (this had a long wood-covered handle, instead of the two squat looped metal handles of the traditional wok) I do find this a good innovation, as is the pouring lip now being introduced in many. But I did find that I couldn't lift the wok and its contents in one hand, so it does have limited value for me.

If you have a small kitchen you'll find a wok invaluable since it can be used to cook all kinds of dishes and can be rinsed quickly, dried and used again.

Seasoning a pressed or rolled-steel wok is all important. When delivered to retail shops, the woks have a coating of lacquer or a protective industrial grease to prevent them rusting. They should first be scrubbed vigorously in boiling water using a washing-up detergent. Then rinsed and drained. Next toss in a handful of coarse salt and rub this over the interior of the wok until you think the coating has been removed. Rinse again well, place the wok on the heat and fill with water. Bring to the boil, boil for a few minutes, then drain. Add about 1 cup of cooking oil and heat until very hot, splashing the oil up the sides of the wok, then drain and rinse in hot water. Dry lightly. Rub the wok dry and shiny using several pieces of crumpled kitchen paper. Before the first few uses, rub the interior briskly with a piece of cut fresh (root) ginger. Chinese cooks have been doing this for centuries and believe that it helps to prevent food from sticking.

After each use the seasoned wok will need only to be well washed with boiling water and scrubbed with a soft brush. Never use detergent, but occasionally use a little pure soap. Rinse well, dry, rub with a lightly oiled cloth or piece of kitchen paper, and hang or store upside down.

Using the wok as a deep-fryer also helps to create an excellent non-stick surface. After frying, drain and thoroughly wash the wok as above. The flavour of the cooking oil permeates the wok as well as protecting the surface. The Chinese have a phrase 'wok-hei', meaning literally wok-air/atmosphere/taste, to describe the indefinable flavour of foods cooked properly in a wok. The measure of a good cook (at home or in a restaurant) lies in how much of this he or she can impart to the dish.

Woks thrive on hard work. Keep your wok in constant use and you'll find that not only do you get better results each time, but you'll soon find the wok indispensable for all types of cooking.

# Wok Accessories

There are a number of simple utensils and accessories that are used with the wok, and which will be required for different recipes in this book.

**The wok 'charn'** is a flat lifting instrument, similar to an egg slice (egg lifter) but with its front edge slightly curved to allow it to follow the interior curve of the wok. The charn is used as the manipulating utensil during stir-frying, but also doubles as a spoon for lifting, stirring, mixing and breaking up ingredients in the pan. It will be necessary to acquire a wooden spatula to use (instead of a metal 'charn') with Teflon-lined woks.

**The steamer rack** is a metal or bamboo rack, shaped to fit inside the wok to support the food to be cooked, either by itself or in a dish, above the bottom of the wok. There should be sufficient space below the rack for water to boil to produce the steam.

**Steaming baskets** Circular baskets of tightly woven cane or bamboo with their own close-fitting lids. Used for cooking Chinese dim-sum and can be used for other steamed dishes. The metal basket-shaped or flat perforated inserts supplied with a pressure cooker can be used in place of steamer racks or steamer baskets. These can also be used as the support for fish during poaching.

**Draining rack/ladle** A perforated metal or wire rack/ladle (skimmer) on which deep-fried foods are rested to drain off excess oil. Ladles can be used to retrieve the food directly from the oil. If unobtainable, use a slotted (perforated) spoon. Draining can also be done on crumpled absorbent paper. Some woks come equipped with a draining rack which clips on the inside rim of the wok. These are acceptable, but the food should not be left on them for a long time as the steam from the dish will cause the crisp surface to soften.

**Wok lid** Without a dome-shaped lid, your wok would be only half-efficient. A lid is used for steaming, poaching, braising and smoking, and in some instances during sautéeing. If your wok is not equipped with a lid, use a large saucepan lid or plate.

**Wok stand** This is a perforated metal ring or wire moulded rack on which to stand the wok between uses. It is particularly useful if the wok is to be used for deep-frying because the full wok of hot oil can be placed safely out of danger on a kitchen bench after use.

**Wok ladle** More like an overgrown spoon than a soup ladle, it is used by the Chinese cook as an all-purpose measuring spoon, mixing bowl for sauce ingredients, tasting spoon, and so on. A soup ladle will suffice.

**Useful extras** include a sturdy but soft scrubbing brush for brushing out the wok during washing; a pair of large wooden cooking chopsticks; a good cleaver; a chopping board; and several heatproof dishes and plates which can be used for steaming. Plus one or two sturdy oven gloves or kitchen cloths. These should always be on hand to use when holding or lifting the wok.

*Steamer rack*

*Wok charn*

*Steaming baskets*

*Draining rack and ladle*

*Wok brushes, chopsticks*

*Wok and lid*

*Wok ladle*

*Wok stand*

*Cleaver, chopping board, oven gloves*

# Stir-frying and Sautéeing

Stir-frying is an energetic and enjoyable cooking method involving active participation from the cook. The wok—although developed by the Chinese as their basic cooking vessel—can be considered as the only really suitable pan for the rapid cooking and constant manipulation that is required for stir-frying. Its uniquely shaped interior allows a smooth sweep across the inside by its accompanying 'charn', which has a curved edge designed to follow the curve of the wok. The rounded bottom of the wok means that it can sit closely over the heat source—particularly over a gas ring—with the heat being distributed evenly up the sides of the pan.

The wok should be well heated before cooking begins, then the cooking medium (vegetable oil, lard or chicken fat) added and heated until a blue haze filling the interior of the wok indicates that it is ready. At this point the food is tossed into the pan and is vigorously stirred with the charn. As the squat looped handles of most woks heat up quickly, wear a sturdy protective glove on the left hand to hold the wok steady, and manipulate the charn with the right hand. The action is fast and continuous: tossing, turning, flipping, stirring, and occasionally shaking the wok with the left hand to aid in the unceasing movements of the wok's contents. Foods to be stir-fried should be prepared in advance and assembled together with the required seasoning and sauce ingredients in the cooking area.

As most Chinese stir-fried dishes comprise a variety of meats and vegetables, it may be necessary to cook these in several batches. Once one lot is done, remove it deftly with the charn to a warmed plate; add the remaining ingredients as dictated by the recipe, cook, then bring the components together.

Sautéeing differs little from stir-frying. Again the ingredients are usually cut into small pieces for quick cooking. Once sautéed and browned on both sides, the ingredients may be removed from the pan and kept warm while the sauce is prepared.

Whereas stir-frying employs mainly vegetable oil as its cooking medium, butter or a mixture of butter and cooking oil are used for sautéeing. As this fat may be too copious to incorporate into the sauce, some or all is drained off before the pan is deglazed with wine or spirits, which bubble up and draw off anything that may have stuck to the bottom of the pan, thus creating the basis for the sauce. This is then thickened, enriched with cream or egg yolks or thinned with stock according to the recipe requirements. The meat may be returned to the pan to be warmed through, but on no account should it be allowed to boil in its sauce or it would toughen.

The sauté method, to achieve perfection, should be done at the very last minute and served immediately on warmed plates. There should be enough room in the pan to allow space between the pieces of meat or they would begin to steam and stew instead of quickly sealing and browning. Yet at the same time, there should be sufficient ingredients in the pan to temper the heat of the fat, which should never be allowed to burn or it would impart a bitter taste to the sauce.

The wok performs most acceptably as a sauté pan. Foods can cover the bottom and extend partially up the smooth sides of the pan where the heat will be maintained evenly. In fact, the flat-based woks now being produced for use on electric cookers are not at all dissimilar to the traditional French sauté pan, the *sautoir*.

# Garlic Prawns
### Gammas Ajillo

SERVES 6

**1 kg (2 lb) large green prawns (raw shrimp),
  in the shell**
**¾ cup (6 fl oz) good olive oil**
**6–7 cloves garlic, sliced**
**1 fresh red chilli, sliced**
**6 fresh basil leaves (optional)**
**salt**

Wash the prawns and dry them on kitchen paper. Heat the oil in the wok, and sauté the garlic and chilli briefly. Add the prawns, and cook on moderate to high heat until the shells turn a bright pink and the prawns are cooked through (about 3 minutes). Add the basil leaves and salt.

Transfer to heated ramekins or other small dishes, and pour on the oil from the pan. Serve piping hot, with crusty bread and lemon wedges.

*Toss prawns in hot oil until they turn pink*   *Pour garlic flavoured oil over prawns and serve*

# Squid Provençale

SERVES 6

This versatile dish can be adapted for scallops, prawns (shrimp) or other seafood, or served as a main course.

**500 g (1 lb) cleaned squid**
**1 large onion**
**1 clove garlic**
**625 g (1¼ lb) tomatoes**
**1 tablespoon butter**
**1 tablespoon olive oil**
**1 bay leaf**
**½ teaspoon dried sage or basil**
**½ teaspoon sugar**
**salt and black pepper**
**2 teaspoons chopped parsley**

Wash squid, dry and cut into rings. Peel and finely chop the onion and garlic. Plunge the tomatoes into a saucepan of boiling water and remove at the count of eight; peel, then chop roughly.

Heat the wok and add the butter and olive oil. When hot, add the squid and sauté until it just turns white, then remove and keep warm. Add the onion and garlic to the wok and sauté gently until lightly coloured. Add the tomatoes and cook on moderate heat for 7 minutes, adding the bay leaf, the sage or basil, the sugar and seasonings. Return the squid to the wok and stir in the chopped parsley. Heat through and serve at once. The squid should not be overcooked or it will toughen.

*Wash and dry squid then cut into rings*

*Plunge tomatoes into boiling water, then peel*

*Sauté squid in olive oil and butter in wok*

*Return squid to tomato mixture in wok just until it heats through*

# Scallops in Pernod

SERVES 4 AS AN APPETIZER, 2 AS A MAIN COURSE

**500 g (1 lb) fresh scallops**
**2 tablespoons butter**
**1 small onion, chopped**
**1 tablespoon flour**
**¼ teaspoon powdered saffron or turmeric**
**½ cup (4 fl oz) dry white wine**
**½ cup (4 fl oz) single (light) cream**
**1½ tablespoons Pernod**
**salt**
**lemon juice**
**chopped parsley**

Wash the scallops. Place them in the wok with water to cover and bring quickly to the boil; drain, cover with cold water and when cool lift out and drain thoroughly.

Wipe out the wok. Heat the butter until bubbling, and sauté the scallops until they turn white and firm, then remove and keep warm.

Add the chopped onion to the wok and sauté until transparent; then sprinkle on the flour and add the saffron or turmeric and cook briefly before adding the wine. Stir well, then simmer until thickened and reduced. Add the cream and mix well, then add the Pernod, with salt and lemon juice to taste. Return the scallops and gently heat through in the sauce. Serve on a bed of white rice with chopped parsley.

*Bring scallops to the boil in a covered wok*

*Add sautéed scallops to the wine sauce and heat*

# Sautéed Liver with Oregano

SERVES 4

**410 g (13 oz) calf's or lamb's liver**
**2 tablespoons olive oil**
**2 tablespoons butter**
**2 shallots (spring onions/scallions), chopped**
**2 cloves garlic, chopped**
**2 teaspoons chopped fresh oregano, or ¾ teaspoon**
    **dried oregano**
**¾ teaspoon salt**
**freshly ground black pepper**
**¼ cup (2 fl oz) dry white wine**
**¼ cup (2 fl oz) thickened (heavy) cream**

Thinly slice the liver, removing any skin and tubes.
Cut into narrow shreds. Heat the oil and butter together
in the wok and sauté the liver quickly until it changes
colour. Add the shallots, garlic and oregano with the salt
and pepper, and continue to sauté until the liver is just
cooked. Remove and keep warm.

    Add the wine to the pan and boil briskly until well
reduced, then stir in the cream and heat through.
Return the liver, toss with the sauce, and serve.

*Thinly slice the liver and cut into shreds*

*Return the sautéed liver to wine and cream sauce*

# African Chicken Livers

SERVES 4

**500 g (1 lb) chicken livers**
**cooking oil**
**1 large onion, chopped**
**2 cloves garlic, chopped**
**1 teaspoon grated fresh (root) ginger**
**1 tablespoon flour**
**⅓ cup (1½ oz) ground roasted peanuts**
**1 large tomato, peeled and chopped**
**6–8 fresh basil leaves, or ¾ teaspoon dried basil**
**1 cup (8 fl oz) chicken stock or water**
**1 teaspoon ground coriander**
**1 teaspoon salt**
**1 teaspoon chopped fresh chilli**
**ground black pepper**
**2 hard-boiled (hard-cooked) eggs**

Cut the livers into bite-sized pieces. Heat about 1½
tablespoons of cooking oil in the wok and gently sauté the
onion, garlic and ginger until lightly coloured. Add the
chicken livers and sauté for about 2 minutes, stirring
frequently. Sprinkle on the flour and leave to colour slightly.
Add the peanuts and stir in; cook briefly. Then add the
chopped tomato and basil and sauté for a further 1 to 2
minutes. Pour in the stock or water, add the spices, chilli and
seasonings; cover the wok and simmer for 5 minutes.

    Peel the eggs and cut them into quarters, stir into the dish
and serve.

*Sauté chicken livers with onion, garlic and ginger*

*Chop fresh basil and peeled tomato*

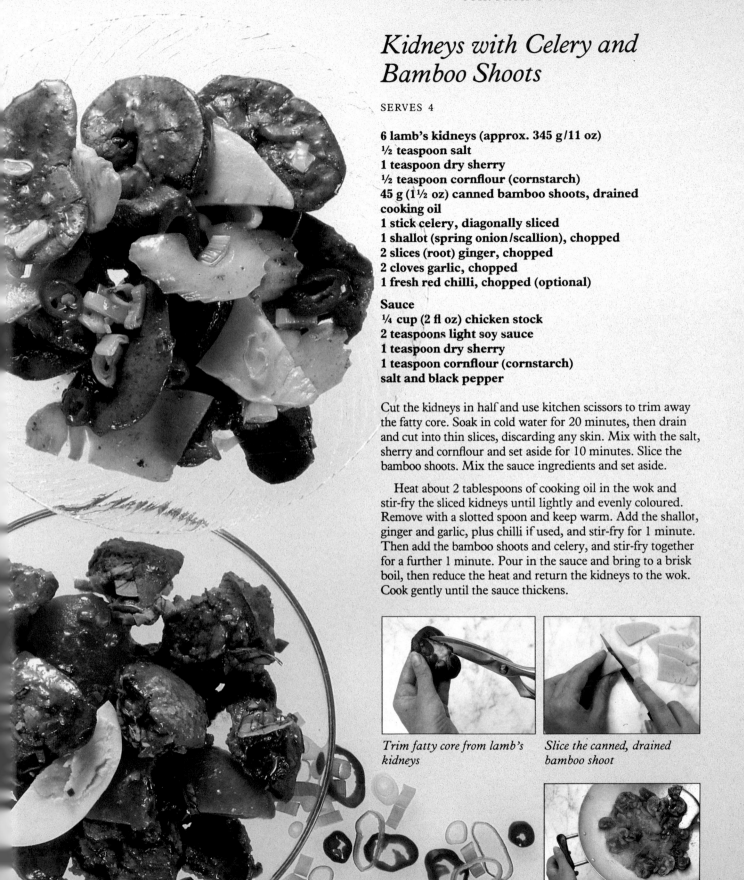

# Kidneys with Celery and Bamboo Shoots

SERVES 4

**6 lamb's kidneys (approx. 345 g/11 oz)**
**½ teaspoon salt**
**1 teaspoon dry sherry**
**½ teaspoon cornflour (cornstarch)**
**45 g (1½ oz) canned bamboo shoots, drained**
**cooking oil**
**1 stick celery, diagonally sliced**
**1 shallot (spring onion/scallion), chopped**
**2 slices (root) ginger, chopped**
**2 cloves garlic, chopped**
**1 fresh red chilli, chopped (optional)**

**Sauce**
**¼ cup (2 fl oz) chicken stock**
**2 teaspoons light soy sauce**
**1 teaspoon dry sherry**
**1 teaspoon cornflour (cornstarch)**
**salt and black pepper**

Cut the kidneys in half and use kitchen scissors to trim away the fatty core. Soak in cold water for 20 minutes, then drain and cut into thin slices, discarding any skin. Mix with the salt, sherry and cornflour and set aside for 10 minutes. Slice the bamboo shoots. Mix the sauce ingredients and set aside.

Heat about 2 tablespoons of cooking oil in the wok and stir-fry the sliced kidneys until lightly and evenly coloured. Remove with a slotted spoon and keep warm. Add the shallot, ginger and garlic, plus chilli if used, and stir-fry for 1 minute. Then add the bamboo shoots and celery, and stir-fry together for a further 1 minute. Pour in the sauce and bring to a brisk boil, then reduce the heat and return the kidneys to the wok. Cook gently until the sauce thickens.

*Trim fatty core from lamb's kidneys*

*Slice the canned, drained bamboo shoot*

*Stir-fry sliced kidneys*

# Chinese Mixed Vegetables

SERVES 4

1 medium-sized carrot
1 stick celery
1 small onion
60 g (2 oz) canned bamboo shoots, drained
90 g (3 oz) canned young corn cobs, drained
6 dried Chinese mushrooms, soaked
12 canned champignons, drained
6 canned water chestnuts, drained
1 medium Chinese cabbage (*bok choy*)
2 slices fresh (root) ginger, shredded
cooking oil

**Sauce**
2 tablespoons water or chicken stock
2 teaspoons Chinese oyster sauce
1 teaspoon dry sherry
1 teaspoon sugar
1 teaspoon cornflour (cornstarch)
¼ teaspoon salt

Peel and thinly slice the carrot, cutting diagonally.
String the celery if necessary and slice similarly.
Peel the onion and cut into wedges from top to root.
Thinly slice bamboo shoots and cut corn into halves.
Drain the mushrooms and remove the stems. Cut the
champignons and water chestnuts into halves.
Thoroughly wash the cabbage and chop roughly.

Heat about 2½ tablespoons of cooking oil in the wok
and stir-fry the raw vegetables first for about 2 minutes,
then add the canned vegetables and ginger and stir-fry until
just tender.

Add the sauce ingredients, premixed, and bring to the boil.
Simmer briefly, and serve hot.

*Thinly slice carrot and celery diagonally*

*Cut onion into wedges and then separate*

*Wash bok choy cabbage then chop roughly*

# Sautéed Spinach with Ham and Hazelnuts

SERVES 6

**500 g (1 lb) fresh spinach**
**2 slices smoked ham or bacon**
**2½ tablespoons butter**
**2 cloves garlic, chopped**
**¼ teaspoon grated nutmeg**
**salt**
**freshly ground pepper**
**2 tablespoons chopped hazelnuts**

Thoroughly wash the spinach, chop roughly and dry in a towel. Finely chop the ham or bacon, and fry in the butter until crisp. Remove, drain and set aside. Add the garlic to the wok and sauté briefly; then put in the spinach, and sauté, stirring frequently, for about 3 minutes. Add the nutmeg and a little salt and pepper, cover the wok and cook on moderate heat for about 5 minutes.

Remove the lid, add the ham and hazelnuts and stir on high heat until any liquid has evaporated. Serve.

Wash spinach and chop roughly

Sauté spinach in garlic and butter in wok

# Sautéed Mushrooms

SERVES 6

**500 g (1 lb) fresh small mushrooms**
**90 g (3 oz) butter**
**2 teaspoons lemon juice**
**salt and black pepper**
**1 teaspoon grated lemon rind**
**2 tablespoons fresh (soft) brown breadcrumbs★**
**1 tablespoon chopped parsley**

Wipe over mushrooms and trim the stalks. Heat the butter in the wok and when foamy, add the mushrooms; sauté on moderate heat until tender. Sprinkle on the lemon juice, and season to taste with salt and freshly ground black pepper.

Mix the lemon rind with the breadcrumbs and parsley. Transfer the mushrooms to a serving plate, and sauté the crumb mixture in the remaining butter for 1 to 2 minutes, then sprinkle over the mushrooms and serve at once.

★ *Make fresh (soft) breadcrumbs by placing day-old bread (crusts removed) in a blender or food processor and chopping briskly.*

Wipe mushrooms with a damp cloth, peel if large

Sauté mushrooms in butter until tender

Sprinkle lemon rind, crumbs and parsley on mushrooms

# Glazed Carrots and Onions

SERVES 6

**12 baby carrots**
**12 small (pickling) onions**
**1 tablespoon butter**
**1 tablespoon brown sugar**
**ground black pepper**

Scrub the carrots without peeling. Peel the onions, trim off the roots but leave the bulb of the root intact. Cut a cross in the bottom of each onion to prevent them falling apart during cooking. Boil the carrots and onions separately in salted water until tender, then drain well.

Melt the butter in the wok on low heat, then add the sugar and the vegetables. Cover and cook gently, shaking the wok from time to time to turn the vegetables, until the sugar becomes a sticky, shiny glaze. Add pepper and serve.

# Stir-fried Broccoli

SERVES 6

**625 g (1¼ lb) fresh broccoli**
**1 clove garlic, crushed**
**½ teaspoon sugar**
**2 tablespoons vegetable oil**
**2 teaspoons dry sherry**
**2 tablespoons water or chicken stock**
**salt**

Wash the broccoli in cold water, drain and cut into flowerets. Place the garlic and sugar in the wok with the vegetable oil, and heat to smoking point. Put in the broccoli and stir-fry for 2 minutes; then splash in the sherry and cook briefly. Add the water or chicken stock, cover the wok and cook on high heat for about 2 minutes, until the vegetables are just tender and most of the liquid has evaporated. Add a little salt to taste and serve at once.

*Trim roots from onions, leaving bulb intact*

*Cut a cross in onion to prevent falling apart*

*Cut the well-washed broccoli into flowerets*

*Add water to the stir-fried broccoli in wok*

*Toss blanched carrots and onions in butter*

# Sautéed Potatoes

SERVES 6

**750 g (1½ lb) potatoes**
**2 tablespoons butter**
**2 tablespoons cooking oil**
**salt and black pepper**
**2 teaspoons chopped parsley**
**⅓ teaspoon chopped fresh rosemary**

Scrub the potatoes and boil in their skins in salted water until just tender. Drain, peel and slice.

Heat the butter and oil together in the wok, and slide in all the potatoes. Sprinkle on a generous amount of salt and pepper and sauté, turning occasionally, until golden.

Sprinkle on the herbs and stir in lightly, taking care not to break up the potatoes. Serve.

Sautéed sliced onion or chopped crisply fried bacon can be added for interest.

# Sour Cabbage with Walnuts

SERVES 4–6

**500 g (1 lb) white cabbage**
**2 tablespoons butter**
**5 black peppercorns**
**2 tablespoons chopped walnuts**
**2 tablespoons white vinegar**
**2½ teaspoons sugar**
**salt**

Rinse, dry and finely shred the cabbage. Heat the butter in the wok and add the lightly crushed peppercorns and the walnuts. Sauté for 1 minute, then add the cabbage and toss until evenly coated with the butter. Sauté, stirring, for about 5 minutes until almost tender.

Add the vinegar mixed with the sugar, and continue to cook and stir until the liquid has evaporated. Add salt to taste, and serve.

*Slice the boiled and peeled potatoes*

*Sprinkle fresh herbs over stir-fried potatoes*

*Finely shred the cabbage using a sharp knife*

*Add cabbage to walnuts and peppercorns in wok*

*Pour in vinegar and sugar and cook until evaporated*

# Stir-fried Beef with Vegetables

*Add soy sauce and flavourings to beef*

*Cut chilli into fine strips, discarding seeds*

*Return beef to stir-fried vegetables in wok*

SERVES 4

**185 g (6 oz) fillet (tenderloin) steak**
**1 tablespoon light soy sauce**
**2 teaspoons dry sherry**
**1 teaspoon cornflour (cornstarch)**
**½ teaspoon sugar**
**1 small green capsicum (bell pepper)**
**1 small red capsicum (bell pepper)**
**1 fresh red chilli**
**1 stick celery**
**1 small carrot**
**60 g (2 oz) canned sliced bamboo shoots, drained**
**2 slices fresh (root) ginger, shredded**
**cooking oil**

**Sauce**
**¼ cup (2 fl oz) chicken stock**
**2–3 teaspoons Hoisin sauce (sweet bean paste)**
**1 teaspoon dry sherry**
**¾ teaspoon cornflour (cornstarch)**

Very thinly slice the beef, cutting across the grain, then cut into narrow strips. This is much more easily achieved if the meat is partially frozen. Place in a dish and add the soy sauce, sherry, cornflour and sugar. Mix well and leave at room temperature for 20 minutes.

Trim away the inner ribs and seed pods from the capsicums and chilli, and cut into narrow strips. Cut the celery, carrot and bamboo shoots into julienne (matchstick) strips. Mix the sauce ingredients together in a small jug and set aside. (Make a paste of the cornflour and some of the liquid before adding to the sauce.)

Heat the wok and add about 2 tablespoons of cooking oil. Stir-fry the beef on high heat until evenly and lightly coloured. Remove and keep warm.

Add the vegetables and ginger and stir-fry until beginning to soften (about 2 minutes), then pour in the sauce and boil rapidly for 30 seconds. Return the beef and continue to cook on high heat until the sauce has thickened. Serve at once.

# Beef and Broccoli on Ribbon Noodles

SERVES 4

90 g (3 oz) fillet (tenderloin) steak
1 teaspoon light soy sauce
1 teaspoon dry sherry
1 teaspoon vegetable oil
1 teaspoon cornflour (cornstarch)
½ teaspoon sugar
pinch of white pepper
90 g (3 oz) broccoli flowerets
2 shallots (spring onions/scallions), shredded
2 slices fresh (root) ginger, shredded
375 g (12 oz) fresh rice ribbon noodles
cooking oil

Sauce
¾ cup (6 fl oz) chicken stock
2–3 teaspoons Chinese oyster sauce
1 teaspoon dark soy sauce (mushroom soy)
1 teaspoon dry sherry
¾ teaspoon sugar
2 teaspoons cornflour (cornstarch)

Cut the steak into paper-thin slices, then into strips and place in a dish with the soy sauce, sherry, oil, cornflour, sugar and pepper. Mix well and leave for 20 minutes.

Rinse the broccoli and drain well. Prepare the shallots and ginger. Pour boiling water over noodles and stir gently until separate.

In a small jug, mix together all the sauce ingredients except the cornflour. Make a paste with a little of the mixture and the cornflour then add it to the sauce and set aside.

Heat the wok and add about ¼ cup (2 fl oz) of cooking oil. Stir-fry the beef until lightly coloured, on high heat; then remove. Add the vegetables to the wok, stir-fry for about 2 minutes, then remove.

Add the noodles to the wok and stir-fry in the oil remaining in the wok until lightly coloured (about 4 minutes). Transfer to a serving plate.

Return the vegetables to the pan and pour in the sauce. Bring to the boil, stirring. Return the meat and heat through, then pour over the noodles and serve at once.

*Cut the steak into paper thin slices*

*Shred ginger and shallots finely*

*Pour boiling water over fresh rice noodles*

*Heat vegetables and sauce before adding meat*

# Orange Lamb Escalopes

SERVES 4

**625 g (1¼ lb) leg of lamb**
**3 large oranges**
**1 tablespoon vegetable oil**
**2 tablespoons butter**
**1 small onion, grated**
**2 teaspoons honey**
**salt and black pepper**

*Cut lamb into escalopes*

*Beat each lightly with the side of a cleaver*

*Sauté lamb escalopes in oil and butter to colour*

Trim the lamb and cut into small thin escalopes. Bat each lightly with the side of a cleaver or a rolling pin to tenderise. Obtain the juice from 2 oranges and finely grate the rind of 1 of them. Slice the third orange thinly and arrange the slices on a serving plate.

Heat the wok and add the oil and butter. Sauté the escalopes for about 2½ minutes until evenly coloured on the surface and almost cooked through. Remove and keep warm.

Add the grated onion to the wok and sauté until lightly coloured. Then add the orange juice, the grated rind and the honey; bring to the boil and simmer for 1 minute. Return the escalopes to the wok to simmer gently, without boiling, for about two minutes. Season with salt and pepper, then transfer to the serving plate and serve hot.

# Pork Fillets in Paprika Cream Sauce

*Flatten slices of pork with heel of hand*

*To crush garlic, sprinkle with salt, mash with knife*

SERVES 4–6

500 g (1 lb) pork fillets
2 tablespoons butter
1 medium onion, finely chopped
1–2 cloves garlic, crushed
1 large rasher bacon, diced
1 small green capsicum (bell pepper), diced
1 small red capsicum (bell pepper), diced
1 teaspoon salt
¼ teaspoon ground black pepper
1½ teaspoons sweet paprika
½ cup (4 fl oz) fresh cream

Very thinly slice the pork, then cut into small escalopes. Sauté in the butter until lightly coloured, then remove and keep warm.

Add the onion and garlic to the wok and sauté until beginning to colour. Add the diced bacon and sauté until crisp. Add the peppers which have been cut into small dice, and sauté until softened (about 2 minutes). Add the remaining ingredients and bring almost to the boil. Simmer gently for 1 minute, then return the pork and heat gently in the sauce for a further 1 to 1½ minutes. Serve immediately.

# Pork Rolls Teriyaki

SERVES 6

6 large thin slices of leg pork (approx. 500 g/1 lb)
6 small leeks or large shallots (spring onions/scallions)
¼ cup (2 fl oz) dry sherry or sake
⅓ cup (3 oz) sugar
⅓ cup light soy sauce
cooking oil
1 cucumber

Bat the pork slices lightly with a rolling pin or meat mallet to tenderize. Trim the leeks or shallots and wash thoroughly. Wrap a slice of pork around each leek or shallot and secure with toothpicks. Mix the sherry, sugar and soy sauce together in a small jug.

Heat the wok and add about 2 tablespoons of cooking oil. Sauté the pork rolls until lightly coloured all over. Add the sauce and simmer gently until reduced to a thick and shiny glaze on the meat. Turn the rolls frequently during cooking to ensure they are evenly glazed.

Cut the cucumber into sticks or small wedges. Transfer the pork rolls to a serving plate and surround with the cucumber.

Pork Rolls Teriyaki can also be served as an appetizer. Make them smaller, using medium-sized shallots and small thin escalopes of pork, and serve one or two per person with cubes of cucumber which have been marinated in a mixture of sugar, salt and vinegar.

*Bat pork slices with a rolling pin to flatten*

*Wrap a slice of pork around quartered leeks*

# Sautéed Veal with Asparagus Sauce

SERVES 4–6

Asparagus gives its distinct flavour and a delicate green colouring to the purée sauce which accompanies tiny escalopes of veal. Try it with fresh asparagus when in season. Or replace the cream with beaten Ricotta cheese to make a slimmers' special.

**500 g (1 lb) veal steak**
**butter for cooking**
**salt and black pepper**
**2 shallots (spring onions/scallions), chopped**
**1 tablespoon flour**
**1 × 340 g (11 oz) can green asparagus**
**2 tablespoons thickened (heavy) cream**
**½ teaspoon lemon juice**

Cut the veal into small thin escalopes and bat each piece with a rolling pin or meat mallet to tenderise.

Heat about 2 tablespoons of butter in the wok and when it begins to foam, put in the veal and saute on both sides until golden. Add the shallots and sauté briefly, then sprinkle on the flour and allow to colour slightly.

Purée half the asparagus with half of the canning liquid in a blender. Pour into the wok and bring almost to the boil. Reduce heat and simmer gently for 5 minutes. Stir in the cream and lemon juice, then transfer to a warmed serving plate.

Rinse out the wok and heat the remaining asparagus in its liquid. Drain and arrange over the meat.

Cut veal into escalopes and beat out to tenderise

Sauté veal in hot butter in wok until golden

Purée the asparagus and add to veal in the wok

# Quick Chicken and Mango Curry

SERVES 2 AS A MAIN COURSE, 4 AS AN APPETIZER

**250 g (8 oz) chicken breasts**
**1 small onion, chopped**
**2 slices fresh (root) ginger, shredded**
**cooking oil**
**1½ teaspoons mild curry powder**
**1 tablespoon flour**
**½ teaspoon salt**
**¾ cup (6 fl oz) water or chicken stock**
**1 tablespoon compressed coconut cream***
**4 slices fresh or canned mango**
**1 tablespoon toasted slivered almonds**

Cut the chicken breasts into cubes after removing skin and any fragments of bone. Sauté the chicken pieces, onion, and ginger in about 2 tablespoons of cooking oil in the wok until the chicken is well coloured and the onion soft. Sprinkle on the curry powder, flour and salt and stir in, then add the water and the grated or finely chopped coconut cream. Bring almost to the boil, then reduce the heat and simmer gently, stirring, until the sauce thickens and the coconut is dissolved. Add the mango and nuts and serve on a bed of white rice.

★ *Or use ¾ cup (6 fl oz) of canned or fresh coconut milk.*

*Cut the boned and skinned chicken into cubes*

*Finely chop the compressed coconut cream*

# Chicken Breasts in Green Peppercorn Sauce

SERVES 4

**2 whole chicken breasts (approx. 750 g/1½ lb)**
**90 g (3 oz) butter**
**2 shallots (spring onions/scallions), chopped**
**2 tablespoons canned green peppercorns,**
**   in their liquid**
**⅔ cup (6 fl oz) dry white wine**
**1 tablespoon lemon juice**
**1 teaspoon Dijon mustard**
**⅓ cup (2½ fl oz) thickened (heavy) cream**
**salt and ground black pepper**

De-bone and skin the breasts and cut into thin escalopes. Melt half the butter in the wok and sauté the chicken until cooked through (about 3½ minutes), then remove and keep warm.

Add the shallots to the wok and cook until softened, then set aside with the chicken.

Add the peppercorns in their liquid and the wine to the wok and bring to the boil. Simmer for about 10 minutes until the wine is well reduced. Add the remaining butter, the lemon juice and mustard, and mix well. Boil gently for 1 to 2 minutes, then stir in the cream and add salt and pepper to taste. Return the chicken and shallots to warm through in the sauce, then serve on a bed of white rice.

*Bone chicken breasts with small sharp knife*

*Cut breast meat into thin escalopes*

*Ingredients for the green peppercorn sauce*

# Turkey and Crab Fricassée in Crêpes

**SERVES 4 AS A MAIN COURSE, 8 AS AN APPETIZER**

Very much a dish for special occasions, these crêpes filled with a rich creamy mixture of turkey and crab can be served as an appetizer or a main course.

**Crêpes**
1¼ cups (5 oz) flour
¾ teaspoon salt
pinch of pepper
2 teaspoons cooking oil or melted butter
1 egg, beaten
1¾ cups (14 fl oz) milk

**Filling**
250 g (8 oz) cooked turkey breast
155 g (5 oz) fresh or canned crabmeat
1 large shallot (spring onion/scallion)
1 tablespoon chopped parsley
1 tablespoon butter
½ teaspoon chicken stock powder
salt and pepper
¼ cup (2 fl oz) dry white wine
1 cup (8 fl oz) single (light) cream or a cream–milk
    mixture
1½ teaspoons cornflour (cornstarch)

**Sauce**
½ teaspoon chicken stock powder
½ cup (4 fl oz) dry white wine
1 bay leaf
⅓ teaspoon salt
90 g (3 oz) butter
2 teaspoons flour
½ cup (4 fl oz) single (light) cream
2 egg yolks, beaten

Sift the flour, salt and pepper into a mixing bowl, add the oil or butter and the egg, and mix in lightly. Then beat in the milk until the batter is the consistency of cream. Set aside for at least 30 minutes.

Shred the turkey. Drain the crabmeat and flake it. Finely chop the shallot. Sauté the turkey, crabmeat, shallot and parsley in the butter for 1 minute. Add the chicken stock, salt and pepper and the wine, and sauté, stirring, until the wine is reduced by half.

Mix the cornflour into the cream and then pour into the wok. Simmer, stirring, until thick, then remove from the heat and keep warm.

To make the sauce, place the chicken stock, wine, bay leaf and salt in a small saucepan; bring to the boil, then simmer until reduced by half. In another saucepan, melt 1 tablespoon of butter, then add the flour and cook until golden (about 1½ minutes). Strain in the reduced stock and wine, mix well and boil gently for 2 minutes. Add the cream and beat on moderate heat until thick and smooth; then add the remaining butter and heat until it begins to melt. Remove from the heat, whisk in the beaten egg yolks and continue to whisk the sauce until thick and smooth. Set aside.

Rinse out the wok and dry it thoroughly. Rub with an oiled cloth, then heat to moderate. Pour in a large spoonful of the batter and tilt the wok so that the batter spreads thinly across the base. Cook until lightly coloured on the underside and beginning to bubble, then turn and cook the other side. Remove and keep warm while the remaining crêpes are cooked. When done, fill the crêpes with the filling and top with a spoonful of the sauce. Serve at once.

*Add milk to batter and beat until smooth*

*Sauté turkey, crabmeat, shallot and parsley in butter*

*Cook large spoonfuls of batter in wok for crêpes*

*Fill crêpes with turkey mixture and roll up*

# Tuna and Peppers in Soy Sauce

SERVES 6

**500 g (1 lb) fresh tuna steaks**
**⅓ cup light soy sauce**
**2 tablespoons sweet sherry or Japanese mirin**
  **(sweet rice wine)**
**1¼ tablespoons sugar**
**1 large green capsicum (bell pepper)**
**cooking oil**

Cut the tuna into 18 pieces and place in a dish. Mix the soy sauce, sherry or mirin and sugar together until the sugar has dissolved. Pour over the fish and marinate for 10 minutes, turning occasionally.

Cut the pepper into squares, discarding the seed pod and cutting away the inner white ribs.

Heat about 2 tablespoons of cooking oil in the wok. Drain the tuna (reserving the marinade) and sauté with the peppers for about 2 minutes. Pour in the remaining marinade, cover the pan and simmer gently for a further 3 minutes. Serve hot with white rice.

To serve as an appetizer or snack, thread the tuna and peppers alternately on short bamboo skewers and cook in the same way.

*Remove skin and cut tuna into 18 pieces*

*Saute marinated tuna and peppers in oil in wok*

# Trout with Almonds

SERVES 4

**4 fresh trout**
**125 g (4 oz) butter**
**½ cup (2 oz) flour**
**salt and black pepper**
**75 g (2½ oz) flaked almonds**
**2 tablespoons lemon juice**
**1½ tablespoons chopped parsley**

Clean the trout and wash thoroughly. Wipe dry, then stand them on a board, opening downwards. Run a rolling pin firmly from tail to head to loosen the bones. Cut through the backbone at each end with a pair of kitchen scissors and carefully pull away the bone. It should lift out in one piece, but check for any stray bones.

Heat half the butter gently in the wok. Season the flour with salt and pepper and use to lightly coat the fish. Fry the trout, two at a time, in the butter for about 2 minutes on each side, until golden and just cooked through. Do not overcook or they would become tough. Lift on to a serving plate and keep warm.

When all trout are cooked, add the remaining butter to the wok and cook the almonds until just golden, then add the lemon juice and parsley and cook briefly. Pour over the fish and serve at once.

*Run a rolling pin firmly from tail to head of fish to loosen the bones*

*Cut through backbone and carefully remove it in one piece*

# Stir-fried Seafood with Vegetables

SERVES 4

**125 g (4 oz) peeled green prawns (raw shrimp)**
**90 g (3 oz) fresh scallops**
**90 g (3 oz) boneless chicken**
**2 teaspoons ginger wine or dry sherry**
**pinch of cornflour (cornstarch)**
**1 medium carrot**
**½ stick celery**
**90 g (3 oz) Chinese cabbage (*bok choy*)**
**6 dried Chinese mushrooms, soaked**
**45 g (1½ oz) canned sliced bamboo shoots, drained**
**1 slice fresh (root) ginger, shredded**
**cooking oil**

**Sauce**
**½ cup (4 fl oz) chicken stock**
**1 teaspoon light soy sauce**
**1 teaspoon dry sherry**
**½ teaspoon salt**
**¼ teaspoon sugar**
**pinch of white pepper**
**1½ teaspoons cornflour (cornstarch)**

*De-vein prawns and cut each into 2–3 pieces*

*Sprinkle chicken and seafood with ginger wine*

*Stir-fry the prepared vegetables in oil in wok*

Wash, dry and de-vein the prawns and cut into 2–3 pieces. Slice the scallops in halves, horizontally. Very thinly slice the chicken, then cut into small squares. Place the scallops and prawns on one side of a shallow dish and the chicken on the other. Sprinkle with the ginger wine, salt and cornflour and leave for 10 minutes.

Peel and thinly slice the carrot. Slice the celery and cabbage. Drain the mushrooms and remove the stems. Mix the sauce ingredients in a small jug and set aside.

Heat the wok and add 2 tablespoons of cooking oil. Stir-fry the prawns and scallops together until they whiten and firm up (about 1½ minutes); remove to a plate. Stir-fry the chicken pieces until white, then set aside with the seafood. Add the vegetables and ginger to the wok, with a little more oil if needed, and stir-fry for about 3 minutes. Pour in the sauce and bring to the boil. Simmer briefly, then return the seafood and chicken to the wok and heat through. Serve hot.

# Masala Prawns

SERVES 4 AS A MAIN COURSE, 6 AS AN APPETIZER

I discovered this tasty treatment for prawns in a tiny fashionable restaurant in Goa. It takes its name from the fragrant Indian curry powder, Garam Masala.

**12 large green king prawns (raw shrimp), in the shell
   (approx. 750 g/1½ lb)
1 teaspoon crushed garlic
1 tablespoon finely chopped parsley
1 tablespoon Garam Masala, or mild curry powder
½ teaspoon salt
1½ tablespoons butter
1½ tablespoons cooking oil
½ cup (4 fl oz) thickened (heavy) cream
salt and black pepper**

Peel the prawns, leaving the tails intact. Slit each one open down the centre backs and remove the vein. Mix the garlic, parsley, Garam Masala and salt together, and press a portion of this into the opening of each prawn.

Heat the butter and oil together in the wok and sauté the prawns, turning several times, until cooked through (about 6 minutes). Transfer to a serving plate.

Pour the cream into the wok and bring to a rapid boil, stirring to incorporate any spices and herbs remaining in the pan. Add salt and pepper to taste, and spoon over the prawns. Serve at once with saffron rice.

*Peel prawns, leaving the tail intact*

*Press seasoning into opening of each prawn*

*Sauté prawns, turning, until cooked*

# Piperade

*Cut raw, smoked ham into dice*

*Add eggs to stir-fried vegetables*

SERVES 4–6

A nourishing and tasty egg and vegetable dish from the Basque Provinces which serves six as an appetizer or four as a main course. Traditionally onion is not included in a Piperade, but you may prefer to add a small finely chopped onion for extra flavour.

**3 green capsicums (bell peppers)**
**¼ cup (4 fl oz) good olive oil**
**500 g (1 lb) ripe tomatoes**
**2 thick slices raw smoked ham, diced**
**salt and black pepper**
**5 eggs, beaten**

Cut the peppers into strips after removing the stems, seed pods and inner ribs. Sauté in the oil for 5 minutes.

Drop the tomatoes into boiling water and remove at the count of eight. Peel, then chop finely. Add to the peppers and cook until the vegetables are tender. Half-way through this cooking, add the ham and salt and pepper to taste. Just before serving, add the eggs, stir in lightly and increase the heat. Cook, stirring, until the egg is just set.

# Deep-frying

The wok has all the features required of a domestic deep-fryer. Its wide top allows plenty of room for the expansion of oil. Its large capacity means that the food for a meal can be fried in one batch, eliminating the problem of keeping some warm and still crisp while the remainder is being cooked.

Its depth means that the oil can be sufficiently deep—a must if one is to achieve perfect deep-frying—and its sloped sides keep the bulk of the oil in the centre directly above the heat source. It is inexpensive to purchase, and inexpensive to use as its unique shape requires a minimum of oil to achieve sufficient depth for use. This is particularly the case when deep-frying only a few items.

Domestic deep-frying continues to be the one really dangerous activity in the kitchen, with countless seriously injured victims treated every year. Deep-frying should always be undertaken with great care. But with a wok, at least one of the major hazards is greatly diminished. The oil heats in the centre of the wok and spreads outwards and upwards towards the rim. When food is added, particularly in the case of potato chips (French Fries)—the most common recorded cause of kitchen fires—which have a high water content, there will be considerable active bubbling of the oil as it burns off the water. These burning hot bubbles spread towards the rim, and there are subjected to cooler air and cooler metal which results in controlling an overflow. Woks are not foolproof, but they are decidedly safer than a straight-sided pan in this respect.

Mastering the art of deep-frying means that a wide variety of interesting new dishes can be included in your family meals. Food that is fried properly should be crisp and dry on the surface, light and moist inside. There shouldn't be an excessive absorption of the cooking fat or oil, and the result shouldn't be heavy, stodgy food high in kilojoules/calories.

### *Deep-frying (continued)*

A fairly large wok is the best. It need not be a good quality one, although a thick base does give best results. The accessories needed for deep-frying are a wire or metal ladle / skimmer or slotted (perforated) spoon; a draining rack or plentiful supply of absorbent paper; and a pair of long-handled tongs or wooden chopsticks to retrieve individual items from the oil. A small chip (French Fry) basket which will fit down into the centre of the oil would be useful for cooking small items, including herbs such as parsley. Some woks come equipped with a wire draining rack which fits on the inner rim of the wok. This can be useful, but is not essential.

Always have the wok lid ready on hand when deep-frying. If the oil should ignite, the flames will be quickly snuffed out when the wok is covered with its lid.

The temperature of deep oil is crucial for successful frying. Temperatures begin at about 175°C (350°F) and range up to 220°C (425°F) for certain foods which require just a quick hot fry. Higher temperatures would burn the oil; lower temperatures would mean that the coating of the food would become oil-saturated and damp.

While a thermometer to gauge the oil temperature would be useful, there is a simple test that can be applied prior to cooking, using day-old bread cut into 2.5 cm (1 in) cubes. To turn the bread a crisp golden-brown, it will require:

90 seconds when oil is at 175°C (350°F/moderate);
60 seconds when oil is at 190°C (375°F/moderately hot);
30 seconds when oil is at 220°C (425°F/hot).

This simple scale can be used for all deep-frying.

The best cooking medium to use for deep-frying are a good-quality cooking (vegetable) oil, peanut oil, lard (pork fat), ghee (clarified butter) or olive oil. Cooking (vegetable) oil is the obvious choice for the majority of dishes as it is relatively inexpensive, has little of its own flavour to impart to the food and no offensive odours. Olive oil is unsuitable for sweets. Lard and ghee are rich and are best for sweet foods. Butter cannot be used for deep-frying as it would burn long before it reached the required temperature.

There should be at least 8 cm (3 in) of oil in the centre of the pan and an allowance of about the same space again above the oil surface for bubbling up and the bulk of the ingredients.

Once the correct temperature has been reached, it is important to retain this throughout the cooking. The temperature will lower slightly at each addition of food, but will then begin to build up again as the food warms.

Avoid attempting to cook too many pieces of food at any one time. This will cause the temperature of the oil to drop dramatically, the food will absorb too much oil, and will stew rather than fry crisply. At any one time, cook only as much as will allow the oil to continue to bubble briskly. It may be necessary to slightly reduce the cooking temperature after the initial 1 or 2 minutes of frying, to prevent a temperature increase which would cause the food to cook too quickly on the outside, making it dark before the inside is cooked through. To achieve crispness, it is often necessary to fry foods a second time. Cook the items once until just cooked through and a light golden colour, then remove and drain well. Allow to cool slightly, and in the meantime reheat the oil to a slightly higher temperature than before. Return the food and fry for about 1 minute.

Frying oils and fats need not be discarded after each use. If correctly cared for and never burnt, they can be re-used many times. After each use, the oil or fat should be strained from the wok through a fine filter or wire strainer. Ideal is the French *chinois*, a conical strainer of fine mesh which is fitted with a filter similar to a coffee filter. A piece of clean muslin or cheesecloth can serve the same purpose.

An easy method for purifying oil is to peel and slice a potato and add the pieces after each use. As the oil or fat cools, the potato is cooked and draws on to itself many of the fine particles that discolour the oil.

When frying oil has become very darkened and discoloured, it is time to discard it and start again. But this can be postponed indefinitely by adding a little new oil at each use. If frying fat smokes excessively when heated, it should be discarded.

Should oil or fat become overheated, the temperature can be reduced quickly to avoid burning by adding a quantity of cold oil or a large spoonful of cold fat and, of course, removing from the heat. Never add water to oil or fat to cool it. In fact, avoid even small splashes of water getting into hot oil or fat because they can splutter dangerously. Ensure that all utensils are thoroughly dried before using in the oil.

Foods should be dried on paper towels before frying, both to avoid spluttering and to ensure that the surface will cook crisp and dry.

There are two main types of foods that are deep-fried: those that are coated, e.g. battered, crumbed, dusted with flour, dipped in beaten egg white; and those that are uncoated, such as whole poultry, whole fish, pastries and potatoes.

The following scale gives temperature requirements and approximate cooking times for various fried foods.

| | | |
|---|---|---|
| **Potatoes** | Chips (French Fries) | 175°C (350°F) for 4–5 minutes, then 220°C (425°F) for 2 minutes |
| | Crisps/Game Chips | 220°C (425°F) for 2 minutes |
| | Shoestring Chips | 175°C (350°F) for 3 minutes, then 220°C (425°F) for 1 minute |
| **Poultry** | Cuts/portions | 190°C (375°F) for 7–8 minutes |
| | Escalopes/croquettes | 190°C (375°F) for 3 minutes |
| | Whole small birds | 190°C (375°F), decreasing, for 6–15 minutes |
| **Fish** | Fillets | 190°C (375°F) for 4 minutes |
| | Fingers | 190°C (375°F) for 2–3 minutes |
| **Scallops** | Whole, coated | 190°C (375°F) for 2–3 minutes |
| **Prawns** | Whole, coated | 190°C (375°F) for 2–3 minutes |
| **Fritters** | | 175°C (350°F) for 3 minutes |

# Iranian Meatballs

MAKES 24

A variety of aromatic spices and fresh herbs combine to make these tempting meatballs from the Middle East.

**500 g (1 lb) minced (ground) beef steak**
**2 slices white bread, crusts removed**
**1 medium onion, grated**
**2 cloves garlic, crushed**
**2 tablespoons chopped fresh herbs (including parsley and mint)**
**½ teaspoon ground allspice**
**1½ teaspoons ground coriander**
**½ teaspoon ground cummin**
**pinch of powdered cinnamon**
**1 teaspoon salt**
**¼ teaspoon ground black pepper**
**2 eggs**
**1½ cups (6 oz) dry breadcrumbs**

Place the meat in a food processor or mincer and chop until smooth and pasty. Remove to a mixing bowl. Cut the bread into cubes, place in the processor and chop into crumbs, then mix with the meat. Add the onion, herbs, spices, salt and pepper, plus one of the eggs. Mix thoroughly, then work to a smooth paste and form into 24 balls.

Beat the remaining egg. Dip the meatballs into the egg and coat with the crumbs. Chill for 45 minutes.

Heat deep oil to moderately hot. Deep-fry the meatballs in several batches until golden brown and cooked through. Drain and serve hot with a garnish of orange slices and sprigs of mint.

*Use wet hands to roll meatballs*

*Coat meatballs with egg and breadcrumbs*

# Camembert Stuffed with Prawns

SERVES 4

**1 Camembert cheese**
**60 g (2 oz) small prawns (shrimp), cooked and peeled**
**1 egg, beaten**
**2 tablespoons dry breadcrumbs**
**½ cup (1½ oz) white sesame seeds**

Cut the Camembert into four wedges. Make a slit in the centre of each and insert several small prawns. Close up and pinch the edges together to reshape.

Dip into the beaten egg and coat lightly with the crumbs, then dip into the egg again and coat with sesame seeds. Place on a tray and refrigerate for 1 hour.

Heat about 3 cups (24 fl oz) of oil in the wok to moderately hot. Put in the Camembert to deep-fry until golden brown. Drain and serve at once on folded paper napkins.

*Insert prawns in wedges of camembert*

*Coat camembert in egg and crumbs then egg and sesame*

# Prawn Toast

MAKES 12

**250 g (8 oz) green prawn
(raw shrimp) meat**
**¾ cup (1½ oz) fresh white
breadcrumbs**
**1 egg white, beaten**
**1½ teaspoons lemon juice**
**¾ teaspoon salt**
**1 teaspoon cornflour
(cornstarch)**
**6 slices fresh white bread**
**1 egg, beaten**
**1 tablespoon white
sesame seeds**

Finely mince (grind) the prawn meat and mix with the breadcrumbs, egg white, lemon juice, salt and cornflour, working to a smooth paste.

Remove the crusts from the bread and cut each slice into halves. Brush one side of each piece with beaten egg and cover with a thick layer of the prawn paste, smoothing the edges with the back of a spoon dipped in cold water. Brush the tops with more beaten egg and sprinkle on a little of the sesame seeds.

Heat deep oil to moderately hot. Deep-fry the prawn toasts, several at a time and fillings downwards, until golden and crisp (about 1¼ minutes). Turn and cook the other sides, then drain well on crumpled absorbent paper before serving. These are particularly good with drinks before dinner.

*Brush bread with egg, coat with the prawn mixture*

*Brush with more egg and dip in sesame seeds*

*Deep-fry prawn toasts, several at a time*

# Scallop Puffs

MAKES 36

155 g (5 oz) fresh scallops
125 g (4 oz) canned champignons, drained
2 tablespoons butter
1 tablespoon grated onion
½ clove garlic, crushed
¼ teaspoon fennel seeds, crushed
2½ tablespoons flour
⅓ cup (2½ fl oz) milk
½ teaspoon hot mustard powder
2 teaspoons lemon juice
185 g (6 oz) frozen puff pastry

Finely chop the scallops and champignons. Sauté in the butter with the onion, garlic and fennel seeds for about 2 minutes. Sprinkle on the flour and continue cooking until lightly coloured.

Heat the milk with the mustard in a small saucepan. Pour into the scallop mixture, and stir on moderate heat until thick and smooth (about 5 minutes), stirring constantly. Remove from the heat, add the lemon juice and leave to cool.

Roll out the pastry fairly thinly and cut into 36 rounds using a 3 cm (1¼ in) circular cutter. Then roll each pastry out individually until very thin and almost transparent. Place a spoonful of the filling in the centre of each pastry and fold over to form crescents. Pinch the edges together, using a little milk or beaten egg to stick them down, if needed.

Heat deep oil to moderately hot and fry the puffs, several at a time, until golden and well expanded. Drain well on paper towels and serve hot.

*Sprinkle flour onto sautéed scallop mixture*

*Roll pastry rounds out until almost transparent*

*Place filling on each round and form a crescent*

*Fry puffs in hot oil and drain on absorbent paper*

# Crisp and Spicy Squid

Clean squid under running cold water

Use a cube of bread to test temperature of oil

SERVES 4

500 g (1 lb) fresh small squid
1 teaspoon crushed garlic
¾ teaspoon ground black pepper
2 egg whites, beaten
¾ cup (3 oz) flour
1¼ teaspoons salt
¾ teaspoon cayenne pepper
1 cup (8 fl oz) olive oil
2 cups (16 fl oz) cooking oil
lemon juice

Clean the squid under running cold water, removing heads, stomach sacs, skin and fins. Rinse well, then cut the tubular bodies into thin rings. Place in a dish, add the garlic and pepper, and mix thoroughly. Set aside at room temperature for 1 hour.

Drain the squid, dry on kitchen paper, then dip into the egg whites. Coat with the flour which has been seasoned with the salt and cayenne pepper.

Heat the olive and cooking oil together in the wok until smoking hot. Reduce heat slightly. Deep-fry the squid in two or three batches until crisp and golden. Drain well and serve hot dressed with lemon juice.

# Stuffed Crab Claws

MAKES 12

12 crab pincers, with meat intact
220 g (7 oz) crabmeat
220 g (7 oz) green prawn (raw shrimp) meat
1½ cups (3 oz) fresh breadcrumbs
2 small eggs, beaten
1 teaspoon salt
¼ teaspoon ground black pepper
2 teaspoons lemon juice
⅓ teaspoon hot mustard powder

Remove the shell from the pincers leaving the meat attached just to the points. Place the other crabmeat, prawnmeat, ½ cup of the breadcrumbs and the remaining ingredients in a food processor or blender and chop to a smooth paste. Form into 12 balls and push a finger through the centre of each. Insert the claw meat into the cavity leaving the pincer protruding. Squeeze the mixture firmly on to the crab claw. You may find it easier to do this if you wet your hands with cold water first. Coat each crab claw with the remaining breadcrumbs.

Heat deep oil to moderately hot. Deep-fry the crab claws, several at a time, until cooked through and golden-brown on the surface (about 2½ minutes). Drain well and serve hot with a chilli or soy sauce dip.

Some crab claws have shell partly removed as shown

Form mixture into balls and insert the crab claw

# Chicken Wings with Plum Sauce

SERVES 6

**6 chicken wings (approx. 500 g/1 lb)**
**1 tablespoon Hoisin sauce (sweet bean paste)**
**2 teaspoons dry sherry**
**1 teaspoon grated fresh (root) ginger**
**1 clove garlic, crushed**
**¾ teaspoon salt**
**1 cup (4 oz) cornflour (cornstarch)**
**1½ tablespoons Chinese plum sauce**

Remove wing tip and keep for soup making

Rub Hoisin sauce mixture evenly over wings

Remove the wing tip and keep for soup making. Wipe the wings with kitchen paper and place in a dish. Add the Hoisin sauce, sherry, ginger, garlic and salt and mix thoroughly, rubbing it evenly into the wings. Leave for 30 minutes to absorb the flavourings, then drain on kitchen paper and coat thickly with the cornflour.

Heat deep oil to fairly hot, then decrease the heat slightly. Put in the wings to deep-fry for about 4½ minutes, turning frequently. Remove with a slotted spoon and arrange on a serving dish. Pour on the plum sauce and serve at once.

Coat wings with cornflour and deep-fry in hot oil

# Stuffed Mini Drumsticks

MAKES 6

**6 chicken wings (approx. 500 g/1 lb)★**
**½ teaspoon grated fresh (root) ginger**
**1 teaspoon finely chopped shallot (spring onion/**
**   scallion)**
**2 teaspoons light soy sauce**
**seasoned cornflour (cornstarch)**
**1 large egg, beaten**
**1½ cups (3 oz) fresh (soft) breadcrumbs**

**Filling**
**90 g (3 oz) finely minced (ground) beef or pork**
**30 g (1 oz) canned water chestnuts, drained**
**1 shallot (spring onion/scallion), chopped**
**¼ teaspoon grated fresh (root) ginger**
**¼ teaspoon crushed garlic**
**2 teaspoons light soy sauce**
**½ teaspoon dark soy sauce (mushroom soy)**
**½ teaspoon dry sherry**
**½ teaspoon sugar**
**2 teaspoons cornflour (cornstarch)**

**Sweet and Sour Sauce**
**1 tablespoon cooking oil**
**1 tablespoon chopped fresh (root) ginger**
**½ teaspoon crushed garlic**
**½ cup (4 fl oz) chicken stock**
**⅓ cup (3 oz) sugar**
**⅓ cup (2½ fl oz) white vinegar**
**pinch salt and pepper**
**1 tablespoon chopped Chinese mixed pickles or**
**   ginger preserved in syrup**
**2½ teaspoons cornflour (cornstarch)**
**red food colouring (optional)**

Scrape away the meat from the bones of the wings, working from the larger end, and push the meat over the smaller end of the bone to form a ball shape with a cavity in the centre top. Place in a dish with the grated ginger, shallot and soy sauce and leave for 20 minutes.

Place the beef or pork, water chestnuts and shallot in a food processor or blender and grind to a smooth paste, then add the ginger, garlic and seasonings. Stir in the cornflour and knead the mixture until smooth and thoroughly amalgamated. Fill into the cavities of the wings and smooth the tops into ball shapes.

Coat lightly with seasoned cornflour, then dip into the beaten egg and coat with the crumbs. Place on a dish and chill for 1 hour before frying to firm the filling and to prevent the crumbs flaking off during cooking.

Heat deep oil to fairly hot and fry the drumsticks, two or three at a time, until golden and cooked through (about 5 minutes). Drain and serve with Sweet and Sour Sauce.

**To make the Sweet and Sour Sauce,** mix together in a clean wok or saucepan the oil, ginger, garlic, chicken stock, sugar, vinegar, salt, pepper and pickles. Blend the cornflour with 1 tablespoon of the liquid from the pickles or ginger and stir in. Bring to the boil and simmer for 2 to 3 minutes. A touch of red food colouring can be added. Serve hot.

★ *Use only the upper (shoulder) joint of the wings, reserving the tips and central joints for another recipe.*

*Use meaty portion of chicken wings*

*Scrape meat away from the bones to form a ball*

*Fill cavity in ball of chicken with beef mixture*

*Dip in egg and coat with breadcrumbs before frying*

# Spring Rolls

MAKES 18

**185 g (6 oz) boneless chicken**
**2 teaspoons light soy sauce**
**2 teaspoons dry sherry**
**¼ teaspoon salt**
**¼ teaspoon sugar**
**¼ red capsicum (bell pepper)**
**75 g (2½ oz) canned sliced bamboo shoots, drained**
**1 medium carrot, peeled**
**75 g (2½ oz) fresh bean sprouts**
**2 cabbage or spinach leaves**
**2 shallots (spring onions/scallions), shredded**
**1 slice fresh (root) ginger, shredded**
**1 pack 20 cm (8 in) frozen spring roll wrappers**

**Sauce**
**¾ teaspoon salt**
**1 teaspoon sugar**
**2 teaspoons light soy sauce**
**2 teaspoons cornflour (cornstarch)**
**1 tablespoon cold water**

Thinly slice the chicken, then cut into narrow shreds.
Place in a dish and add the soy sauce, sherry, salt and sugar,
mix well and leave for 20 minutes.

Remove stem, seed pod and inner ribs from the capsicum.
Shred the capsicum, bamboo shoots and carrot into julienne
(matchstick) strips. Rinse and thoroughly drain the bean
sprouts. Finely shred the cabbage or spinach leaves.

Heat about 2 tablespoons of cooking oil in the wok and
stir-fry the chicken until white. Remove and keep warm.
Add the vegetables, shallots and ginger to the wok, and stir-
fry until tender. Return the chicken and add the premixed
sauce ingredients. Simmer, stirring until there is no liquid in
the bottom of the pan, then transfer to a plate to cool.

Thaw the spring roll wrappers under a cloth, then separate
and keep covered. To wrap, place a portion of the filling in
the centre of each wrapper; fold over one corner and shape
the filling into a roll, fold in the two sides, then roll up
tightly. Dip the end in water and stick down. If water is not
effective in sticking down the ends, make a paste by boiling
1 tablespoon of cornflour (cornstarch) with about ⅓ cup
(2½ fl oz) of water, and brush this on.

Heat oil for deep-frying in a clean wok and fry several rolls
at a time in moderately hot oil, for about 3 minutes. Drain
on crumpled absorbent paper and keep warm while the
remainder are being cooked. Serve hot with Sweet and Sour
Sauce (see page 41) or dips of light soy and chilli sauces.

*Place filling on spring roll wrapper and fold*

*Roll up and dip end in cold water to seal*

*Spring rolls can be made in two sizes*

# Pork Wontons

MAKES 48

410 g (13 oz) fatty pork
45 g (1½ oz) fresh bean sprouts
60 g (2 oz) canned water chestnuts, drained
2 shallots (spring onions/scallions), chopped
1 tablespoon finely chopped parsley
½ teaspoon grated fresh (root) ginger
1½ teaspoons salt
¼ teaspoon pepper
2 teaspoons sugar
1 tablespoon light soy sauce
2 teaspoons cornflour (cornstarch)
48 frozen or fresh wonton wrappers (approx. 345 g/
    11 oz)

Cut the pork into small cubes and place in a food processor or blender; grind to a smooth paste. Finely chop the bean sprouts and chestnuts, and add to the pork with the remaining ingredients — excluding the wrappers, of course. Mix thoroughly, kneading until fairly smooth. Wrap in a piece of plastic film and chill for 1 hour.

Thaw and separate the wonton wrappers and cover with a cloth. To fill, place a teaspoonful of the mixture in the centre of a wrapper and pinch the edges together encasing the filling. The edges must be brushed with a little water in order to seal.

Wontons can be made in a variety of shapes. The *Purse* has its edges all drawn up together into a point at the centre top. The *Goldfish* is formed by folding three edges one over the other to give a smooth ball shape on top, and the remaining corner is fluted out and down to form the tail. To make a *Swimming Fish*, pull three corners up and over the filling in the centre, and the remaining corner is fluted upwards and outwards in a tail shape. The *Bon Bon* is rolled around the filling and the ends are twisted to resemble a wrapped sweet/candy.

Heat oil for deep-frying until fairly hot. Fry about eight at a time, until golden (about 2½ minutes). Drain and serve hot on a bed of Fried Chinese Cabbage (see page 46).

*Purse-shaped and goldfish wontons*

*Swimming fish and Bon Bon wontons*

# Vegetable Curry Triangles
## Samoosas

MAKES 36

2 medium potatoes
90 g (3 oz) peas
1 medium onion
90 g (3 oz) cauliflower, chopped
1 tablespoon butter
2 teaspoons Garam Masala, or hot curry powder
1 tablespoon chopped parsley
1 teaspoon chopped fresh mint, or a pinch of
   dried mint
2 teaspoons lemon juice
1 teaspoon salt
1 pack 25 cm (10 in) frozen spring roll wrappers

Boil the potatoes in their jackets in lightly salted water, then peel and cut into dice. Boil the peas until tender, then drain. Finely chop the onion.

Sauté the onion and cauliflower in the butter until tender and lightly coloured. Add the potatoes and peas and sauté briefly. Then add the spices, herbs, lemon juice and salt, and mix well. Transfer to a plate and leave to cool.

Thaw the spring roll wrappers under a cloth, then separate and keep covered. When ready to use, cut into strips about 4.5 cm (1¾ in) wide.

To fill, turn over one end to form a triangular pouch and fill with about 2 teaspoons of the filling. Wrap up the pastries, keeping to the triangular shape and enclosing the filling. Brush the ends with cold water and press into place.

Heat deep oil to hot. Deep-fry the pastries, several at a time, until golden. Lift out with a slotted spoon and drain well before serving hot. Tomato sauce spiked with chilli makes a tasty accompaniment.

*Separate the thawed spring roll wrappers*

*Form a triangular pouch and spoon in filling*

*Fold up pastries*

# Curry Puffs Taj Mahal

*Knead pastry gently until smooth*

*Place filling in centre of pastry square, fold over*

*Press edge with fork to seal and decorate*

*Fold points in to form an envelope*

MAKES 18

**Pastry**
**1 cup (4 oz) flour**
**¼ teaspoon salt**
**1 large egg, beaten**
**1 tablespoon butter or margarine**
**lukewarm water**

**Filling**
**250 g (8 oz) lean minced (ground) beef**
**1 medium cooked potato**
**¼ cup (1½ oz) cooked peas**
**1 medium onion, chopped**
**2 cloves garlic, crushed**
**½ teaspoon grated fresh (root) ginger**
**2½ teaspoons hot curry powder**
**¼–½ teaspoon chilli powder**
**¾ teaspoon salt**
**pinch of black pepper**
**1 tablespoon chopped fresh mint or parsley**
**1 tablespoon lemon juice**

Sift the flour and salt into a mixing bowl and make a well in the centre. Add the egg and the softened butter or margarine, and work in lightly. Add just enough water to make a reasonably firm dough. Lift the dough on to a lightly floured board and knead gently until smooth. Wrap in plastic wrap and chill until needed.

Sauté the beef in about 2 tablespoons of butter until lightly coloured. Stir it continuously to separate the pieces. Add the potato and peas and sauté lightly; then add the onion, garlic and ginger and continue to cook for 5 to 6 minutes. If the mixture begins to catch on the bottom of the pan, splash in a very little cold water from time to time. Add the curry and chilli powders and the salt and pepper and cook for 1 to 2 minutes more. Remove from the heat and stir in the chopped herbs and lemon juice. Spread on a plate to cool.

Knead the dough again lightly, then roll out into a large thin sheet, trim the sides straight and cut into eighteen 7.5 cm (3 inch) squares. Divide the filling between the pastries. Fold each in halves to give triangular shapes. The edges should be brushed with beaten egg (use the reserved egg white) or milk to help them stick. Use the points of a fork to indent a design around the edges.

Fold the two extreme points over to meet and slightly overlap in the centre front, and use a little more egg or milk to stick down. The finished pastry should resemble an open envelope.

Heat deep oil to moderately hot. Deep-fry the pastries, several at a time, until golden. Lift out with a slotted spoon and drain well. Serve hot with sweet chutney, mint sauce or tomato sauce.

# Fried Chinese Cabbage

This crisply fried green vegetable can be served as a side dish or used as a delicious edible garnish with fried appetizers such as Prawn Toast (page 37) or Pork Wontons (page 43).

**12 large leaves of Chinese cabbage (*bok choy*)**
**¾ teaspoon sugar**
**1 teaspoon sesame oil**
**2 teaspoons white sesame seeds**

Finely shred the bok choy leaves, discarding any stems, and place them in a frying basket. Heat deep oil to moderately hot and insert the basket. Fry until the bok choy is bright green and rustles when the basket is shaken over the oil. Drain well on kitchen paper and place in a serving dish. Combine the remaining ingredients, pour over the bok choy and mix thoroughly.

Shredded silver beet leaves can be used instead of cabbage, but they will require less sugar.

Finely shred the leaves of the bok choy

Plunge the bok choy into oil until bright green

# Onion Rings

SERVES 4

**2 medium onions**
**1 cup (8 fl oz) milk**
**1 cup (4 oz) flour**
**1 egg, beaten**
**¼ teaspoon salt**

Peel the onions and slice reasonably thinly. Separate into rings and place in a dish. Pour on the milk and leave for 1 hour. The milk will draw off some of the strong flavour from the onion.

Drain the onions thoroughly, reserving the milk. Mix the milk with the flour, egg and salt, beating to a smooth batter.

Heat deep oil in the wok. Dip the onion rings one by one into the batter and place in the oil. Cook only eight to ten at a time, turning when the underside has become golden. Drain thoroughly. Keep warm while the remainder are cooked. These can be made a short time in advance and quickly re-fried in very hot oil just before serving to ensure crispness.

Separate the thinly-sliced onion into rings

Pour milk over onions to remove strong flavour

# Pommes Noisette

SERVES 6

**750 g (1½ lb) large potatoes**
**seasoned flour**

Peel and wash the potatoes and use a melon scoop to cut out balls with a diameter of about 2 cm (¾ in). Parboil in lightly salted water, then drain thoroughly and leave to cool and dry. Coat lightly with the seasoned flour.

Heat deep oil to moderately hot. Deep-fry the potato balls until golden (about 5 minutes). Remove and leave to cool slightly while the oil reheats. Return the potatoes to the oil and fry for a further 1 to 1½ minutes until very crisp and golden on the surface. Drain on kitchen paper, sprinkle with salt and serve.

*Cut potatoes into balls with melon baller*

*Dry parboiled potatoes thoroughly before frying*

# Crisp Zucchini (Courgette) or Eggplant (Aubergine) Slices

SERVES 4

This is a delicious way to use up older vegetables.

**1 large zucchini (courgette), or 1 to 2 long thin**
**eggplants (aubergines)**
**1 cup (4 oz) flour**
**salt and pepper**
**2 tablespoons grated Parmesan cheese**

Thinly slice the vegetables without peeling and spread on a board or tray. Sprinkle generously with salt and leave for 1 hour. The salt will draw off the bitter juices.

Rinse the vegetables thoroughly, then dry on a cloth. Season the flour with salt and pepper and coat the vegetables.

Heat deep oil to fairly hot. Deep-fry the vegetables in two or three batches until crisp and golden. Drain and transfer to a serving dish, sprinkle on the cheese and serve at once.

*Thinly slice zucchini or eggplant*

*Sprinkle salt on zucchini to remove bitter juices*

# Chicken Kebabs

MAKES 12

This simplified version of Indonesian Satay can be served as an appetizer or main course. Cook it without the chilli powder as a treat for a children's party.

**345 g (11 oz) chicken breasts, boneless**
**2 teaspoons lemon juice**
**1 teaspoon mild curry powder**
**pinch of chilli powder or cayenne pepper**
**¼ teaspoon salt**

**Batter**
**1 cup (4 oz) flour**
**1 cup (8 fl oz) water**
**½ teaspoon salt**
**1 teaspoon baking powder**
**½ teaspoon mild curry powder**
**¾ cup (3 oz) dry breadcrumbs**

Skin the chicken breasts and rub with a mixture of the lemon juice, curry and chilli powder (or cayenne) and the salt. Place on a covered plate and set aside at room temperature for 10 minutes to absorb the flavours.

Cut the chicken meat into 12 strips and thread each strip on to a bamboo or metal skewer. Mix the batter ingredients, except breadcrumbs, together in a bowl. Spread the crumbs on a plate.

Heat deep oil to moderately hot in the wok. Dip the chicken into the batter, then coat with crumbs. Place in the deep oil to fry for about 2½ minutes or until cooked through and golden brown on the surface. Serve hot with wedges of lemon and a sweet chutney.

*Rub chicken meat with juice and curry powder*

*Cut chicken into strips and thread on skewers*

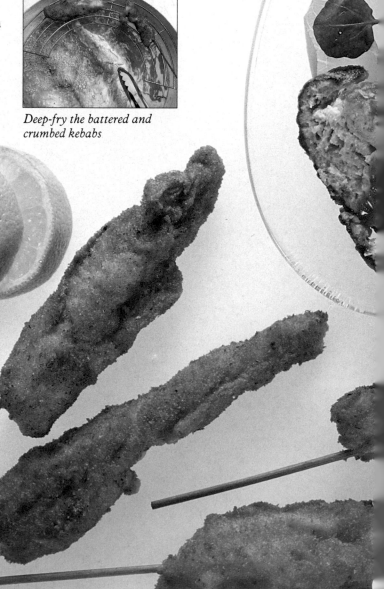
*Deep-fry the battered and crumbed kebabs*

# Chicken Supreme

SERVES 4 AS A MAIN COURSE, 8 AS AN APPETIZER

1–1¼ kg (2½ lb) roasting chicken
250 g (8 oz) peeled green prawns (raw shrimps)
2 shallots (spring onions/scallions)
45 g (1½ oz) canned water chestnuts, drained
1 slice fresh (root) ginger
2 teaspoons ginger wine or dry sherry
¾ teaspoon salt
cornflour (cornstarch)

**Sauce A**
½ cup (4 fl oz) chicken stock
2 teaspoons oyster sauce
½ teaspoon light soy sauce
½ teaspoon sugar
1 tablespoon cooking oil
¾ teaspoon cornflour (cornstarch)

**Sauce B**
½ cup (4 fl oz) bottled Chinese plum sauce
2 teaspoons tomato sauce (ketchup)

Clean the chicken, cut in half and trim away the backbone. Use a short, narrow-bladed knife to carefully de-bone the chicken, leaving just the first section of the wing bone in position. Cut off the two lower joints of the wings, and the drumsticks and thighs and reserve for another recipe. Set the chicken aside.

De-vein the prawns and place in a food processor or blender with the trimmed shallots, water chestnuts, ginger, wine or sherry and salt. Chop to a smooth paste.

Dust the meaty side of the chicken halves with cornflour, then coat each with the prawn paste. Coat with more cornflour, then cover with a piece of plastic wrap and chill for at least 1 hour, to help hold the filling on the chicken during cooking.

When ready to cook, heat deep oil to moderately hot. Coat the chicken again with cornflour, brushing off the excess. Place in the oil to fry gently for about 15 minutes. Turn the chicken using tongs to avoid breaking the skin. Drain well.

Serve with Sauce A or Sauce B, according to which would best suit other dishes on the menu. Bring Sauce A ingredients to the boil in a small saucepan and simmer, stirring, until thickened. Heat Sauce B just to boiling point. The sauce may be poured over the chicken or served separately.

*Carefully remove bones from the half chicken*

*Cut off wings, thigh and drumstick*

*Spread with prawn mixture, coat with cornflour*

# Fisherman's Basket

SERVES 6

3 fish fillets (approx. 315 g/10 oz)
125 g (4 oz) scallops
12 green prawns (raw shrimp), in the shell (approx.
    375 g/12 oz)
12 fresh oysters
1 large bunch parsley
cornflour (cornstarch)
2 lemons

**Egg White Batter**
1 cup (4 oz) flour
½ cup (2 oz) cornflour (cornstarch)
1 teaspoon salt
2 teaspoons baking powder
1 cup (8 fl oz) water
2 large egg whites

**Tartare Sauce**
1 cup (8 fl oz) mayonnaise
1 teaspoon dry mustard
½ teaspoon dried tarragon
2 teaspoons chopped chives
2 teaspoons chopped capers
2 teaspoons chopped gherkins (dill pickles)
1 teaspoon mashed anchovy (optional)
salt and pepper

*Prepare the seafood and
parsley*

*Fold whipped egg whites into
the batter*

*Plunge parsley into hot oil for
20 seconds*

Cut each fish fillet into four pieces. Remove the roe from the
scallops, if necessary. Peel the prawns, leaving the tails intact;
de-vein and rinse in cold water. Remove oysters from the shell
and rinse in lightly salted water. Wash the parsley, shake out
excess water then wrap in a kitchen towel until needed.

To make the egg white batter sift the flours, salt and baking
powder into a mixing bowl and add the water. Beat until
smooth, then set aside for about 15 minutes. Add a very
little more water if the mixture seems too thick; it should
be the consistency of thick (heavy) cream.

Whip the egg whites to soft peaks and fold carefully into
the batter. Once the eggs have been incorporated, the batter
should be used at once.

Heat deep oil to moderate. Pat the seafood pieces
dry with kitchen paper and coat lightly with cornflour,
shaking off excess. Dip into the batter and deep-fry,
several pieces at a time, until cooked through,
crisp and golden. Drain on crumpled absorbent paper.
When all are cooked, arrange in small (breadroll) baskets
lined with paper napkins or on a pretty serving dish.

Place the parsley in a frying basket and plunge into the
oil to cook for about 20 seconds until bright green and crisp.
Drain well and arrange around the seafood, adding several
lemon wedges to each basket. Serve hot with Tartare Sauce.

To make the Tartare Sauce, mix the ingredients together
and allow to stand for about 3 hours before serving. Store in
an airtight jar in the refrigerator.

# Prawns in Wine and Chilli Sauce

SERVES 2

12 green prawn cutlets (raw shrimps, peeled),
  approx. 250 g/8 oz★
5 cloves garlic, sliced
3 slices fresh (root) ginger, shredded
1 large red chilli, sliced
2 shallots (spring onions/scallions), sliced
2 egg whites
½ cup (2 oz) cornflour (cornstarch)

Sauce
2 teaspoons light
  soy sauce
2 teaspoons sugar
¼ cup (2 fl oz) dry sherry
¼ cup (2 fl oz) chicken
  stock
small pinch of salt
1 teaspoon cornflour
  (cornstarch)

*Mix sauce ingredients*

*Flour prawns, dip in batter then in cornflour*

*Deep-fry prawns until crisp, then drain*

Wash the prawns and dry thoroughly; set aside. Mix the sauce ingredients.

Sauté the garlic, ginger, chilli and shallots in about 2 tablespoons of cooking oil for 1 minute. Add the premixed sauce ingredients and bring to the boil. Stir on moderate heat for 2 minutes, then set aside.

Beat the egg whites to soft peaks, then fold in half the cornflour. Dust the prawns lightly with the remaining cornflour, shaking off the excess.

Heat deep oil to hot. Dip the prawns into the batter, then coat them lightly with the remaining cornflour. Deep-fry, six at a time, until crisp. When all are done, reheat the oil and deep-fry the prawns again for about 30 seconds. Drain well.

Pour off the oil and reheat the wok. Add the sauce and bring to the boil, then pour over the prawns and serve.

★ *Peeled prawns, de-veined and then slit open down the centre back and pressed open.*

# Honey Chilli Fish

SERVES 6 AS AN APPETIZER, 4 AS A MAIN COURSE

**500 g (1 lb) white fish (sea perch/sea bass)**

**Beer and Wine Batter**
**1 cup (4 oz) flour**
**2 tablespoons cooking oil**
**30 ml (1 fl oz) dry white wine**
**¾ cup (6 fl oz) beer**
**¾ teaspoon salt**
**3 egg whites**

**Honey and Chilli Sauce**
**2½ tablespoons clear honey**
**2 teaspoons chilli sauce**

Cut the fish into fingers of about 9 × 4 cm (3½ × 1½ in). Beat the flour, oil, wine, beer and salt together and set aside.

Heat deep oil to hot in the wok. Beat the egg whites to soft peaks and fold into the batter. Dip the fish into the batter, lower carefully into the hot oil and deep-fry until crisp and golden (about 2½ minutes), turning once. Remove on a slotted spoon and drain on absorbent paper. Serve immediately all the fish is cooked, with accompanying Honey and Chilli Sauce.

To make the Honey and Chilli Sauce, heat the honey and chilli sauce together in a small saucepan. Serve hot in a small jug, or pour the sauce over the fish just before serving.

*Cut fish into finger-sized pieces*

*Dip fish into beer batter and lower into hot oil*

# Sweet and Sour Prawns

SERVES 4

**375 g (12 oz) prawn (shrimp) cutlets★**
**2 tablespoons cornflour (cornstarch)**
**½ small carrot**
**5 cm (2 in) piece of cucumber**
**⅓ stick celery**
**¼ red capsicum (bell pepper) or chilli pepper**
**1 shallot (spring onion/scallion)**
**2 slices fresh (root) ginger**
**1 canned pineapple ring, drained**

**Batter**
**½ cup (2 oz) flour**
**1 teaspoon baking powder**
**½ teaspoon salt**
**½ cup (4 fl oz) water**
**2 egg whites**

**Sweet and Sour Sauce**
**2 tablespoons cooking oil**
**½ cup (4 oz) sugar**
**½ cup (4 fl oz) white vinegar**
**¼ cup (2 fl oz) pineapple juice**
**1 tablespoon cold water**
**2½ teaspoons cornflour (cornstarch)**

Wipe the prawns on kitchen paper and dust lightly with cornflour. Set aside. Peel and shred the carrot and cucumber, discarding the cucumber seeds. Scrape and shred the celery. Trim away the seed pod and inner ribs of the pepper or chilli and cut into long narrow shreds. Trim and shred the shallot and ginger. Cut the pineapple into small cubes. Beat together the batter ingredients, except the egg whites, and set aside.

Heat the oil for the sauce in a wok or saucepan and add the sugar. Cook on fairly high heat until the sugar is dissolved and becomes dark and syrupy. Add the remaining ingredients, well-mixed, and bring to the boil. Simmer, stirring, until the sauce thickens. Add the carrot and cucumber and boil until softened. Then add the remaining vegetables to the sauce and simmer for 1 minute. Set aside.

Rinse out the wok, if used for the sauce. Heat deep oil to hot. Beat the egg whites to soft peaks and fold into the batter. Dip the prawns into the batter, then place in the hot oil to cook until crisp, puffed and golden (about 1¾ minutes). Lift out with a slotted spoon and drain well on kitchen paper. Drain the wok, reheat the sauce if necessary and pour over the prawns. Serve at once.

\* *Peeled raw prawns (shrimp) with the tail shell intact; deveined, and butterflied (cut down centre back and pressed open).*

*Dust prawn cutlets lightly with cornflour*

*Cut all the vegetables into shreds*

# Noodle Baskets

MAKES 6 INDIVIDUAL SERVING BASKETS

Chinese egg noodles can be used to make edible food containers, which look particularly effective with seafood dishes such as Sweet and Sour Prawns (previous recipe) or Stir-fried Seafood with Vegetables (page 29).

**5 cakes of thin egg noodles (approx. 250 g/8 oz)**

Soak the noodles in cold water until they separate. Drain very thoroughly by spreading on several layers of kitchen paper and covering with more paper.

Select two wire strainers, one slightly larger than the other. Dip them in deep oil and shake to remove most of the oil. Divide the noodles into six equal portions. Line the larger strainer with a portion of the noodles and press the smaller strainer inside to form the noodles into a nest or basket shape.

Heat deep oil to hot. Place the strainers in the oil, holding the two handles firmly together. Cook for about 2 minutes until the smaller basket can be lifted out without disturbing the noodles, then continue to cook until golden and crisp. Lift out, drain well, then upturn on to absorbent paper. Tap the bottom of the strainer to release the basket. Leave to drain upside down until needed.

Unused noodle baskets can be stored in an airtight container and warmed in a moderate oven when needed. To use, stand the baskets on a plate and surround with parsley or celery leaves. Fill with the prepared dish and serve.

*Line strainer or potato nest maker with noodles*

*Half way through cooking remove the top strainer*

# Almond Fingers

MAKES 36

**1 cup (4 oz) flour**
**¼ teaspoon salt**
**1 cup (8 fl oz) water**
**2 tablespoons butter**
**2 large eggs**
**2 tablespoons ground almonds**
**1½ cups (12 oz) sugar**
**1¼ cups (10 fl oz) water**
**1½ teaspoons orange or rose flower water**

Sift flour and salt on to a piece of greaseproof paper. In a
closed wok, bring the 1 cup of water to the boil with the
butter, then quickly shoot in all the flour and beat with the
handle of a wooden spoon until the mixture leaves the sides
of the wok and becomes a shiny smooth lump. Cook gently
for about 5 minutes, stirring from time to time, then remove
from the heat and transfer to a mixing bowl. Leave to partially
cool, then gradually beat in the eggs and the almonds.
Set aside for 10 minutes.

In a saucepan boil the 1¼ cups of water with the sugar,
stirring just until the sugar dissolves. Simmer for about
10 minutes until the syrup begins to look sticky, but has not
taken on any colour. Remove from the heat and add the
flower water. Set aside to cool.

Rinse the wok and add clean cooking oil for deep-frying.
Heat to moderate. Roll the dough into small finger-shapes,
using wet hands to prevent sticking. Slide, several at a time,
into the oil and cook for 8 to 10 minutes, until golden and
puffed out. It is essential that the oil is not too hot or the
pastries would cook too quickly on the outside and remain
soft and sticky inside.

Remove with a slotted spoon and transfer to the cool
syrup. As each batch of pastries is cooked, remove the
previous batch from the syrup and place on a serving plate.

When done, the pastries can be garnished with finely
chopped walnuts, toasted almonds or pistachios. Or they
can be sprinkled with a mixture of cinnamon and sugar just
before serving.

*Add flour all at once to
boiling water and butter*

*Stir with spoon handle until
mixture forms ball*

# Easy Doughnuts

MAKES 12

**2 cups (8 oz) flour**
**2 teaspoons baking powder**
**¼ teaspoon ground cinnamon**
**⅓ cup (3 oz) caster (powdered) sugar**
**2 teaspoons melted butter**
**1 egg, beaten**
**lukewarm milk**

Sift the flour, baking powder and cinnamon into a mixing
bowl. Add the sugar and melted butter and stir in lightly.
Then add the egg and enough milk to make a soft dough.
Roll out on a lightly floured board until it is about 1 cm
(⅓ in) thick.

Cut into rounds using a floured scone or biscuit (cookie)
cutter of about 8 cm (3 in) diameter, then use a smaller cutter
to make a hole in the centre of each.

Heat clean deep oil to moderately hot. Fry the doughnuts,
several at a time, until golden, turning once. When evenly
coloured and cooked through, remove and drain thoroughly.
Cook the 'holes' until golden and serve with the doughnuts.

They can be rolled in a mixture of 2 tablespoons caster
sugar and 1½ teaspoons ground cinnamon before serving.
Serve at once.

*Cut dough into rounds with
two cutters*

*Deep-fry doughnuts until
golden*

# Toffeed Apple

SERVES 6

This is a highly regarded Chinese dessert. Not easy to get right, but worth a try!

**2 large green (cooking) apples**
**1½ tablespoons white sesame seeds**
**cooking oil**

**Batter**
**1 cup (4 oz) flour**
**2 tablespoons cornflour (cornstarch)**
**1 egg, beaten**
**1 cup (8 fl oz) water**

**Toffee**
**1 tablespoon sesame oil**
**2 cups (1 lb) sugar**

Peel, core and slice the apples and set aside. Mix the batter ingredients together, beating until smooth.

Heat clean deep oil to hot. Dip the apple pieces one by one into the batter and fry until crisp. Drain. When all the apple pieces have been done once, reheat the oil and fry again for 1½ minutes to crisp the batter; drain well and place on a plate near the cooking area.

Drain the wok and wipe out. Add the ingredients for the toffee and heat, stirring occasionally, until the sugar has melted and turned to a light toffee colour. Add the sesame seeds and the apple pieces, and turn quickly but carefully in the toffee until evenly coated. Remove to the plate, which should be lightly oiled to prevent sticking.

Serve at once with a dish of iced water. To eat, each piece of apple should be separated from the others and dipped into the water, where the toffee will solidify.

*Dip apple slices into batter*

*Return fried apple to hot oil briefly to crisp*

*Turn apple in toffee then add sesame seeds*

# Shallow-frying

Shallow-frying, as an alternative to deep-frying, is usually applied to the kind of foods that require careful handling during cooking, as well as lower temperatures. Food such as uncoated fish can fall apart if allowed to bubble freely in deep oil, whereas with the confines of shallow oil, they may cook gently and be turned without damage. Thin and tender escalopes and cutlets coated with crumbs would become tough and chewy in deep oil, whereas shallow-frying in butter and oil will make them crisp on the surface, yet moist and flavourful inside.

A mixture of equal amounts of cooking (vegetable) oil and butter, or olive oil and butter, is the most common cooking medium for shallow-frying. The oil allows the butter to heat beyond its normal tolerance, bringing to the dish a richness of flavour that frying in oil alone would not provide. However, oil or butter alone can be used.

Shallow-frying is done in varying depths of fat, depending on the food being cooked. It can be as little as a thin spread in the bottom of the wok, or up to a depth of 5 cm (2 in) in the centre of the wok (using more than that would be considered deep-frying).

The fat should be heated to moderate, at which point butter will begin to foam, or oil will respond to the bread test (see the introduction to deep-frying). When the food is added to the wok, the heat can be slightly increased to counteract any cooling off caused by the cold food. When the surface is sealed on all sides, the heat can be lowered so that the food may cook gently without becoming too dark on the surface. It is essential that the wok is not crowded during shallow-frying or the food will begin to 'stew' instead of frying crisply. If you are cooking too much food to fit comfortably into one wok, shallow-fry in batches, keeping the cooked food warm in the oven. Or better still, use two woks.

Tongs, wooden spoons or large metal spoons are used to turn the food, and care should be taken not to break the surface of the food—whether it be a crumb or flour coating, or its own skin — as this will allow the natural juices of the meat, for example, to escape into the cooking fat. The result will be a lowering of cooking temperature, dryness of meat and an excessive absorption of the cooking fat.

Sweet foods should be cooked in new oil, clean lard (pork fat), butter, or ghee (clarified butter); and this can then be reserved for cooking future sweet dishes. If strong flavours of spices, liqueurs, etc., have been imparted to the oil, use it again only for cooking dishes whose flavour will be enhanced by it.

Similarly, fats used for cooking seafoods should be reserved exclusively for cooking other seafoods, as they will become strongly flavoured by the seafood.

Fried foods should be well drained before serving. Crumpled absorbent kitchen paper is ideal for this. Take two or three sheets and bunch them lightly together, place in the bottom of a suitable dish and transfer the food from the oil to the paper to drain for a couple of minutes.

If crisply fried foods, such as crumb- or batter-coated meats or seafoods are to be kept warm in the oven, prop the oven door slightly ajar so that steam can escape. This should help to retain their crispness.

# Empanadas

MAKES 24

**280 g (9 oz) frozen puff pastry**
**250 g (8 oz) smoked fillet of cod or haddock**
**2 cups (16 fl oz) milk**
**2 tablespoons lard or olive oil**
**1 medium onion, finely chopped**
**1 green capsicum (bell pepper), diced**
**185 g (6 oz) raw smoked ham, diced**
**1 tablespoon flour**
**¼ teaspoon cayenne pepper**

Thaw the pastry and cover with a cloth until needed.
Place the fish in the wok and add the milk. Cover and
simmer gently until the fish is tender (about 8 minutes),
then drain, reserving the milk. Skin the fish and flake it.
Pick out any bones.

Heat the lard or oil in a clean wok and sauté the onion,
pepper and ham for about 4 minutes. Add the flour, cayenne
pepper and fish, and sauté for a further 1 to 2 minutes.
Then add just enough of the reserved milk to make the
mixture into a thick sauce. Season with salt if needed,
then remove from the wok and spread on a plate to cool.

On a lightly floured board, roll out the pastry thinly.
Cut into 24 rounds of about 10 cm (4 in) diameter.
Place a spoonful of the filling in the centre of each pastry
Dip a pastry brush into the remaining milk, and damp the
edges of the pastry. Fold over into crescent shapes and pinch
the edges together. Press the point of a fork around the edges
to seal and decorate.

Shallow-fry the pastries in about 4 cm (1½ in) of
moderately hot cooking oil with a little olive oil added for
flavour, until the pastries are golden brown and slightly
puffed. Serve hot.

*Place fish in wok and pour*
*milk over it*

*Heat lard or oil and sauté*
*onion, pepper and ham*

*Fold pastry over filling to*
*form a crescent*

# Chicken 'Hedgehogs'

MAKES 18

**250 g (8 oz) boneless chicken**
**1 egg**
**2 tablespoons flour**
**2 teaspoons sugar**
**2 teaspoons light soy sauce**
**2 teaspoons dry sherry**
**¼ teaspoon salt**
**250 g (8 oz) rice vermicelli**

Cut the chicken into cubes and place in a food processor or mincer (grinder) with the egg, flour, sugar and other seasonings. Chop (grind) to a smooth paste, then transfer to a dish. Cover with plastic wrap and chill for 20 minutes.

Form the mixture into 18 balls. Finely crush the vermicelli. Roll each ball in the noodles to coat.

Heat about 2.5 cm (1 in) cooking oil in the wok to moderate. Fry the 'hedgehogs' about six at a time, until golden and cooked through (about 3 minutes). Drain well and serve warm with soy sauce or sweet chilli sauce.

*The rice vermicelli*

*Crush vermicelli in a plastic bag*

# Danish Meatballs
## *Frikadeller*

MAKES 36

**250 g (8 oz) lean veal**
**250 g (8 oz) lean pork**
**125 g (4 oz) beef steak**
**125 g (4 oz) cooked ham**
**1 medium onion**
**1 teaspoon salt**
**½ teaspoon ground black pepper**
**1 large egg**
**1 teaspoon bicarbonate of soda**
**¼ cup (1 oz) dry breadcrumbs**
**⅓ cup cream**

**Dill Mayonnaise**
**2 tablespoons mayonnaise**
**1½ tablespoons thickened (heavy) cream**
**¾ teaspoon dried dill tips**
**½ teaspoon caraway seeds**

*Roll meat mixture into balls and flatten tops*

*Fry about eight meatballs at a time until golden brown all over*

Finely mince (grind) the meats, ham and onion, and then add the remaining ingredients, mixing thoroughly. Chill for 1 hour, then make 36 meatballs and flatten each slightly.

Heat about 2.5 cm (1 in) cooking oil or a mixture of butter and oil in the wok to moderate. Fry the meatballs, about eight at a time, until golden brown (about 5 minutes). Drain well. Serve warm or cold with Dill Mayonnaise.

To made the Dill Mayonnaise, mix the ingredients together about 2 hours before use.

# Stuffed Peppers

SERVES 4

**2 large green or red capsicums (bell peppers)**
**250 g (8 oz) finely minced (ground) pork**
**30 g (1 oz) canned water chestnuts, drained**
**1 shallot (scallion/spring onion)**
**½ teaspoon salt**
**pinch of ground black pepper**
**1½ teaspoons dry sherry**
**cornflour (cornstarch)**

**Batter**
**½ cup (2 oz) flour**
**¼ cup (1 oz) cornflour (cornstarch)**
**1½ teaspoons baking powder**
**½ cup (4 fl oz) water**
**2 egg whites**

Cut each of the peppers into quarters, lengthways, trimming away the inner ribs and the seed stem. Place the pork in a mixing bowl. Finely chop the water chestnuts and shallot, and add to the pork with the salt, pepper and sherry. Mix thoroughly, then use to fill each piece of pepper. Smooth the tops and set aside.

Mix the batter ingredients, except the egg whites, thoroughly. When ready to cook, whisk the egg whites until they stand in soft peaks, then fold into the batter.

Coat the stuffed peppers lightly with cornflour, then dip into the batter. Shallow-fry several at a time in about 5 cm (2 in) of moderately hot oil until golden, puffed out and cooked through (about 5 minutes). Drain well and serve hot.

*Quarter peppers and remove ribs*

*Spread pork filling on pepper quarters*

*Dip into cornflour, then batter*

# Potato Pancakes

## Latkes

SERVES 4

These crisp potato pancakes are delicious as a breakfast dish, a snack or to accompany a main course. They are also worth trying as a dessert, served hot with warmed blueberries or fresh strawberries and lashings of sour cream.

**700 g (1⅓ lb) grated raw potato**
**¼ cup (1 oz) flour**
**2 large eggs, beaten**
**salt and black pepper**

Select large potatoes, peel and rinse thoroughly, and soak them in cold water for about 45 minutes. Drain and grate fairly coarsely, then squeeze out as much water as possible.

Add the flour and eggs to the potato, and season generously with salt and pepper.

Heat about 1.5 cm (½ in) butter and cooking oil in the wok. When foamy, add a large spoonful of the batter, pressing it into a pancake shape with the back of the spoon. Cook three or four Latkes at a time, depending on the capacity of the wok, until a deep golden colour underneath. Turn and cook the other sides until well coloured. Remove and drain on absorbent paper.

*Grate the soaked potatoes coarsely*

*Squeeze out as much water as possible*

# Sweetcorn Fritters

MAKES 24

Sweetcorn fritters are a must with Chicken Maryland (page 68) but also make interesting snacks or starters, particularly before a curry dinner.

**440 g (14 oz) frozen or canned sweetcorn kernels**
**1 medium onion, grated**
**⅓ cup (1½ oz) flour**
**1½ tablespoons cornflour (cornstarch)**
**2 teaspoons baking powder**
**¾ teaspoon chilli sauce or powder**
**1 teaspoon salt**
**pinch of ground black pepper**
**1 egg, beaten**

Thaw frozen corn, or drain canned corn, then place in a food processor or blender and crush lightly. Add the onion, after draining thoroughly. Add the flour, cornflour, baking powder, chilli and seasoning; mix well, then add the egg. The mixture should be quite moist, yet thick enough to hold together in the oil. Leave for 10 to 15 minutes.

Heat about 4 cm (1½ in) oil in the wok to fairly hot. Drop in teaspoonfuls of the mixture and leave to cook until crisp and golden. Reduce the heat after the first few minutes to ensure that the fritters cook through before becoming too dark on the outside. Drain on crumpled absorbent paper and serve hot or warm. Hot chilli sauce, soy sauce or chutney are ideal accompaniments.

*Add beaten egg to sweetcorn mixture*

*Drop spoonfuls of mixture into hot oil*

# Lamb Noisettes in Curry Sauce

SERVES 4

**8 lamb loin chops (approx. 625 g/1¼ lb)**
**2 cloves garlic, crushed**
**1 small onion, grated**

**Coconut Curry Sauce**
**1 large onion, grated**
**½ teaspoon grated fresh (root) ginger**
**2 cloves garlic, crushed**
**2 teaspoons mild curry powder**
**1 tomato, chopped**
**1¼ cups (10 fl oz) coconut milk**
**2 tablespoons desiccated (shredded) coconut**
**1 teaspoon sugar**
**½ teaspoon sugar**
**pinch of ground black pepper**

Remove the bones from the chops and roll each into a noisette. Tie firmly with string, or pass a short bamboo or metal skewer through each to hold it in shape. Rub with the garlic and onion, and set aside.

Heat about 1½ tablespoons of cooking oil in the wok and sauté the onion, ginger and garlic. Add the curry powder and sauté briefly. Add the tomato and coconut milk, bring to the boil and simmer for about 10 minutes. Then add the desiccated coconut and the seasonings and simmer for a further 5 to 6 minutes. Pour into a jug and set aside.

Rinse out the wok and dry thoroughly. Add about 4 cm (1½ in) oil to the wok and heat to moderate. Fry the noisettes in two or three batches until cooked through and golden brown (about 5 minutes), turning once. Remove and drain.

Pour off the oil. Return the noisettes to the wok and pour on the sauce. Heat gently for about 5 minutes, then serve.

*Remove bones from chops and roll up*

*Rub the noisettes with garlic and onion*

*Add tomato and coconut milk*

# French Cutlets with Mustard and Artichoke Sauce

SERVES 6

*Flatten the cutlets with a rolling pin*

*Add half the artichokes to sauce in a blender or food processor*

*Fry the cutlets in the butter and oil*

12 French cutlets (approx. 850 g/1¾ lb)★
½ cup (2 oz) seasoned flour
1 large egg, beaten
2 tablespoons milk
1¼ cups (5 oz) dry breadcrumbs
2½ tablespoons butter
2 tablespoons cooking oil

**Sauce**
1½ tablespoons butter
1 medium onion, finely chopped
2 tablespoons flour
1 tablespoon Dijon mustard
¾ cup (6 fl oz) water
½ cup (4 fl oz) dry white wine
1 × 400 g (13 oz) can artichoke hearts, drained
¾ cup (6 fl oz) thickened (heavy) cream
2 teaspoons chopped parsley
salt and pepper

Bat the meaty part of each cutlet with the end of a rolling pin or a meat mallet to flatten and tenderise. Coat the cutlets lightly with the flour seasoned with salt and pepper. Beat the egg and milk together. Dip the cutlets into this mixture, then coat with the breadcrumbs. Chill for about 45 minutes to set the crumbs.

To make the sauce, melt the butter in the wok and add the onion. Cook over low heat until the onion is transparent. Then sprinkle on the flour and cook briefly. Add the mustard and stir well, then add the water and wine and bring to a brisk boil. Whisk to remove any lumps, reduce heat and simmer for 1 to 2 minutes. Pour into a blender or food processor, add half the artichokes, and blend to a smooth purée. Return the purée to the wok. Heat through, add the cream and parsley, and season to taste. Pour into a sauce boat and keep it warm.

Rinse the wok and add the butter and oil. Heat until the butter foams, then add half the cutlets and fry for about 3 minutes on each side until golden brown. Lift out with a slotted spoon and arrange on a warmed serving plate. Keep warm while the remaining cutlets are cooked. Drain the wok. Thinly slice the remaining artichoke hearts. Heat a little extra butter in the wok over low heat and lightly cook the artichoke hearts just until they are warmed through. Arrange over the cutlets and pour on a small amount of the sauce. Serve the remaining sauce separately.

★ *French cutlets are lamb loin cutlets (chops) well trimmed and with the end of the bone stripped of its meat. The bones should be decorated with a poultry (paper) frill or covered with aluminium foil before serving.*

# Pork Chops in Fruit Sauce

SERVES 6

**6 pork chops (approx. 1 kg/2 lb)**
**salt and black pepper**
**1 egg white, beaten**
**1 cup (4 oz) dry breadcrumbs**
**125 g (4 oz) butter**

**Fruit Sauce**
**1 cup (6 oz) canned black cherries or plums**
**2 cloves**
**½ teaspoon ground cinnamon**
**grated rind (peel) of ¼ lemon**
**¼ cup (2 fl oz) Madeira or Port**

*Brush chops with egg white and coat with crumbs*

*Fry 2–3 chops at a time until golden*

Season the chops with salt and pepper. Brush with the egg white and coat with the crumbs, shaking off excess. Chill for 1 hour to set the crumbs.

Melt the butter in the wok. Fry the chops, two or three at a time, until cooked through and golden brown (about 7 minutes). Lift out and keep warm while the remaining chops are cooked.

*Pour cherry sauce over chops in wok*

Blend half the fruit with the juice to a smooth purée, then heat in a small saucepan with the spices, lemon rind and wine. Simmer for 2 to 3 minutes.

When all the chops are cooked, return them all to the wok, pour on the sauce and remaining fruit and simmer gently for 4 to 5 minutes before serving. Alternatively the sauce may be served separately.

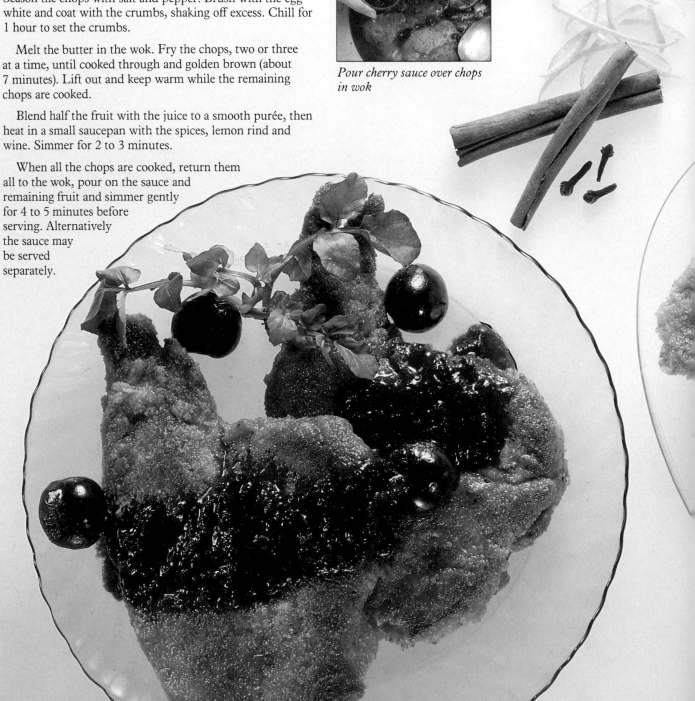

# Wiener Schnitzel

SERVES 6

This dish may be served in the traditional manner, by arranging overlapping steaks on a serving plate and garnishing them with lemon wedges, onion rings and drained capers. Alternatively, it may be served with Lemon and Mustard Mayonnaise and slices of fresh avocado.

6 veal steaks (approx. 625 g / 1 ¼ lb)★
ground black pepper
1 ½ tablespoons lemon juice
½ cup (2 oz) seasoned flour
2 large eggs, beaten
2 cups (8 oz) dry breadcrumbs

Lemon and Mustard Mayonnaise
3 egg yolks
salt and pepper
1 ½ tablespoons lemon juice
1 ¾ tablespoons Dijon mustard
125 g (4 oz) butter

Pound the steaks out very thinly, using a meat mallet or rolling pin and taking care not to break through at any point. Grind a little black pepper over one side of each steak and sprinkle on the lemon juice. Leave for about 15 minutes.

Coat the steaks lightly with the seasoned flour, shaking off the excess. Dip into the beaten egg, then coat with the crumbs. Arrange side by side on a tray and chill for 1 hour to set the crumbs.

Heat about 90 g (3 oz) butter with about ⅓ cup (2½ fl oz) olive or cooking oil in the wok. Fry the schnitzels three at a time, for about 3 minutes on each side. Drain thoroughly and keep warm while the remaining steaks are cooked.

To make the Lemon and Mustard Mayonnaise, beat the egg yolks lightly with a dash of salt and pepper. Add the lemon juice and the Dijon mustard, and mix well. Place the bowl on a rack in the wok, and pour almost-boiling water into the wok.

Cut the butter into small cubes and slowly beat into the sauce, beating between each addition. When all the butter has been added, continue to beat gently until the mayonnaise is thick and creamy. Do not allow the water to boil, or the mayonnaise will curdle. Serve at once.

★ *Buy rump or topside veal steaks that have been cut wide and thinly.*

*Season veal with pepper*

*Take care with coating when removing schnitzels*

*Gradually beat butter into sauce*

# Fritto Misto Milanese

**SERVES 4**

Many are familiar with the seafood version of Fritto Misto containing slivers of crumbed fish, rings of calamari, scallops and prawns, but this version from Milan is equally appetizing, with its combination of tender chicken breasts, brains and sweetbreads complemented by vegetables and soft Mozzarella cheese.

**200 g (6½ oz) lamb's brains**
**200 g (6½ oz) sweetbreads**
**200 g (6½ oz) chicken breasts**
**1 medium zucchini (courgette)**
**60 g (2 oz) fresh mushrooms**
**90 g (3 oz) Mozzarella cheese**
**½ cup (2 oz) seasoned flour**
**2 eggs, beaten**
**1 cup (4 oz) dry breadcrumbs**
**juice of 1 lemon**
**1 tablespoon chopped parsley**

Soak the brains and sweetbreads separately in cold water for 1 hour. Drain, and pick off any membranes and specks of blood. Place in separate saucepans of cold water and add a dash of salt and lemon juice. Bring slowly to the boil and simmer for 15 to 18 minutes, then remove from the heat and leave to cool in the water. Remove and drain well.

Remove skin and any fragments of bone from the chicken and cut the meat into eight strips. Cut the brains and sweetbreads into eight pieces each. Wash, dry and slice the zucchini. Peel the mushrooms and trim the stems. Cut the cheese into four slices.

Prepare the seasoned flour (by adding salt and pepper). Coat the vegetables and meat with the flour; dip into the beaten egg; then coat with the crumbs. Arrange on a tray and chill for 1 hour.

Heat about 125 g (4 oz) butter and 2 to 3 tablespoons of olive oil in the wok to moderate. Fry the crumbed meats and vegetables in small batches until tender. Remove with a slotted spoon, drain well on kitchen paper and arrange in groups on a well-heated serving plate. Keep warm until all ingredients have been cooked.

Drain the wok and wipe out any crumbs that have flaked off. Return the fat to the wok and reheat. Add the lemon juice, heat until very foamy, then pour over the dish and garnish with the parsley. Serve at once.

*Remove membranes from sweetbreads and brains*

*Cut the cooled sweetbreads and brains into pieces*

*Coat vegetables and meat with flour*

# Chicken Akbar

**SERVES 4**

**90 g (3 oz) Filo pastry (4 sheets)**
**250 g (8 oz) boneless chicken breasts**
**2 shallots (spring onions/scallions), chopped**
**1 small clove garlic, crushed**
**1 tablespoon pine nuts**
**1 tablespoon slivered almonds**
**1½ tablespoons sultanas (seedless raisins)**
**2 tablespoons butter**
**1 teaspoon mild curry powder**
**1 tablespoon flour**
**¼ cup (2 fl oz) chicken stock**
**¼ cup (2 fl oz) thickened (heavy) cream**
**salt and black pepper**

Cover the pastry with a kitchen towel until needed.
Finely shred the chicken and mix with the shallots and garlic.

Sauté the nuts and sultanas with the chicken in the butter
until the chicken is lightly coloured. Sprinkle on the curry
powder and cook briefly, then add the flour and cook for
about 1 minute. Add the chicken stock and bring almost to
the boil, stirring. Add the cream and seasoning and simmer
gently for about 2 minutes, until the sauce is thick.
Remove from the heat and leave to cool slightly.

Fold each sheet of pastry in half to give rectangular shapes
about 20 × 18 cm (8 × 7 in). Brush with melted butter.
Place one-quarter of the filling on each piece of pastry,
fold in the sides and then fold the pastry over the filling to
completely enclose it. Press the edge to seal.

Heat about 1 cm (⅓ in) of mixed butter and oil in the
wok and gently fry the pastries, two at a time, until golden.
Drain and arrange on a serving plate. Serve hot.

*Fold pastry in half and brush with butter*

*Place filling on pastry, fold in sides*

*Fold pastry over to enclose filling, press edges*

# Chicken Maryland

SERVES 4–6

While this name now seems to be applied to chicken in many forms—crumbed and deep-fried, roasted or even battered and shallow-fried—the traditional recipe for Chicken Maryland states that it should be coated generously with well-seasoned flour, fried in bacon fat and served with accompanying fried bananas, grilled bacon and corn fritters. A tasty cream sauce made with the pan drippings is served with it.

**1–1¼ kg (2½ lb) chicken**
**¾ cup (3 oz) flour**
**1 teaspoon salt**
**½ teaspoon black pepper**
**½ teaspoon oregano**
**½ teaspoon powdered**
**   sage**
**185 g (6 oz) bacon fat or**
**   lard (pork fat)**

**Sauce**
**1½ tablespoons flour**
**1 cup (8 fl oz) milk**
**2 tablespoons thickened**
**   (heavy) cream**
**1 egg yolk, beaten**
**salt and black pepper**

**Accompaniments**
**1–2 rashers (slices) streaky**
**   (fat) bacon per serving**
**sweet corn fritters**
**   (see page 61)**
**2–3 ripe but firm bananas**

*Cut chicken into serving portions*

*Shallow-fry chicken pieces, several at a time, in wok until evenly coloured*

Cut the chicken into serving portions, trimming away and discarding the backbone. Mix the flour, salt, pepper and herbs together. Dip the chicken into the milk to be used for the sauce, then coat thickly with the seasoned flour.

Melt the fat or lard in the wok and when moderately hot, fry the chicken, several pieces at a time, until well and evenly coloured on the surface. Put in all the chicken, cover the wok and continue to cook gently for about 18 minutes, turning from time to time. Drain off the fat and remove the chicken.

Wipe out the wok to remove any flecks of burnt flour, then return about 2 tablespoons of the fat to the wok, to make the sauce. Add the flour, cook until lightly coloured, then add the milk and stir on moderate heat until thickened. Remove from the heat. Beat the cream and egg yolk together and stir into the sauce. Add salt and pepper to taste, then return to low heat, stir until the sauce thickens, and keep it warm.

While the chicken is being cooked, grill the bacon separately until crisp. Corn fritters can be made in advance and reheated in the oven. Slice the peeled bananas, coat with the remaining seasoned flour and fry in the remainder of the cooking fat until crisp on the surface and soft inside. Surround the chicken with its accompaniments and serve hot with the sauce drizzled over.

# Sweet and Sour Chicken Drumsticks

Cut capsicums into small squares

Coat marinated drumsticks thickly with cornflour

SERVES 3–6

**6 chicken drumsticks (approx. 500 g/1 lb)**
**2 teaspoons light soy sauce**
**2 teaspoons dry sherry**
**1 teaspoon sugar**
**1 cup (4 oz) cornflour (cornstarch)**
**½ medium onion, thinly sliced**
**½ stick celery, thinly sliced diagonally**
**1 small carrot, thinly sliced**
**½ red capsicum (bell pepper)**
**30 g (1 oz) canned sliced bamboo shoots, drained**
**3 slices fresh (root) ginger, shredded**

**Sauce**
**¼ cup (2 fl oz) chicken stock**
**¼ cup (2 fl oz) white vinegar**
**¼ cup (2 oz) sugar**
**½ teaspoon salt**
**1 teaspoon chilli sauce or ground black pepper**
**2–3 drops red food colouring**
**1 tablespoon cornflour (cornstarch)**

Prick the drumsticks all over and place in a dish. Add the soy sauce, sherry and sugar and rub thoroughly over the drumsticks. Leave for 20 minutes.

Prepare the vegetables. Cut the pepper into small squares, discarding the seed pod, stem and inner ribs. Mix the sauce ingredients together in a jug and set aside.

Heat about 5 cm (2 in) cooking oil in the wok to moderately hot. Drain the drumsticks and coat thickly with the cornflour, shaking off the excess. Fry until golden brown and cooked through (about 5 minutes), turning occasionally using tongs to prevent breaking the coating. Remove and drain on absorbent paper.

Pour off the oil, rinse out the wok and return about 2 tablespoons of the oil. Stir-fry the vegetables together for about 2½ minutes, then pour in the sauce and bring to the boil. Simmer, stirring, for 2 to 3 minutes. Return the drumsticks, and heat through. Serve at once.

# Thai-style Fish with Ginger Sauce

SERVES 6

This sauce is also suitable for serving with other seafoods or with plain fried chicken.

**6 white fish fillets (sea perch, coral trout/red emperor), approx. 700 g/1⅓ lb**
**¾ cup (3 oz) seasoned flour**

**Ginger Sauce**
**½ cup (3 oz) ginger preserved in heavy syrup**
**¼ cup (2 oz) sugar**
**¼ cup (2 fl oz) white vinegar**
**1 tablespoon light soy sauce**
**1 cup (8 fl oz) water**
**pinch of salt**
**1 tablespoon cornflour (cornstarch)**
**2–3 shallots (spring onions/scallions), finely chopped**

*Remove skin from fish fillets and coat with flour*

*Fry the floured fish 2 pieces at a time*

Dry the fish with kitchen paper and coat lightly with the seasoned flour. Set aside.

Finely chop the ginger. Place it in a wok or saucepan with the remaining sauce ingredients and bring to the boil, stirring. Simmer for about 3 minutes, then set aside.

Wipe out the wok, if used, and add about 4 cm (1½ in) cooking oil. Fry the fish two pieces at a time, for about 3 minutes on each side, until cooked through. Lift out and drain. Cook the remaining fish. Arrange on a serving plate and pour on half the sauce. Serve the remaining sauce separately. Garnish with chilli if liked.

# Pan-fried Fish with Green Mayonnaise

*Sprinkle lemon juice over fish and coat with flour*

*Combine green mayonnaise ingredients*

SERVES 4

**8 small fillets of fish**
**½ cup (2 oz) flour**
**½ teaspoon salt**
**¼ teaspoon white pepper**
**1 tablespoon lemon juice**
**2–3 tablespoons chopped parsley**
**1 lemon, thinly sliced**

**Green Mayonnaise**
**2 hard-boiled eggs**
**1 cup (8 fl oz) mayonnaise**
**1 teaspoon Dijon or other French mustard**
**1 tablespoon finely chopped raw spinach**
**1 tablespoon finely chopped parsley**
**1 tablespoon drained finely chopped capers**

Dry the fish on kitchen paper. Mix the flour, salt and pepper together on a piece of paper. Sprinkle the lemon juice over the fish on both sides, then dip into the seasoned flour to coat evenly. Shake off the excess.

Heat about 2 tablespoons of butter and 1 tablespoon of cooking oil in the wok and fry two pieces of fish for about 2 minutes on each side, then for a further 1 minute on the first side; remove and keep warm. Add additional butter and oil to the pan and fry the remaining fish.

Arrange the fish on a serving plate. Dip the sliced lemon into the chopped parsley and arrange over the fish. Pour on any butter that remains in the pan and serve at once.

To make the Green Mayonnaise, peel and finely chop the eggs or push through a wire sieve. Mix with the remaining sauce ingredients. If preferred, the sauce may be gently warmed before use. Leftover mayonnaise can be stored in an airtight jar in the refrigerator for up to a week and can be served with fish and shellfish.

# Prawns Stuffed with Crab

SERVES 4

**625 g (1 ¼ lb) green prawn cutlets (raw shrimps, peeled)\***
**2 teaspoons butter**
**1 tablespoon finely chopped celery**
**1 tablespoon finely chopped mushroom**
**1 teaspoon finely chopped fresh chilli**
**1 tablespoon flour**
**¼ cup (2 fl oz) milk**
**1 ½ teaspoons lemon juice**
**⅓ teaspoon salt**
**1 × 200 g (6 ½ oz) can crab, drained**
**2 ½ cups (5 oz) fresh (soft) breadcrumbs**
**2 egg whites, or 2 whole eggs**

Heat the butter in the wok and sauté the celery, mushroom and chilli briefly, then sprinkle in the flour and cook for about 30 seconds. Add the milk and bring to the boil; stir until the mixture is thick. Remove from the heat and add the lemon juice and salt. Stir in the crabmeat and 1 tablespoon of the crumbs, and mix thoroughly to smooth any lumps. Cool. Stuff each of the prawn cutlets with a spoonful of the filling, re-forming them to their original shape. Chill for 1 hour.

Beat the egg whites or eggs in a dish. Spread the crumbs on a piece of paper.

Heat about 2.5 cm (1 in) clean oil in the wok. Dip the prawns in the beaten egg and coat evenly with the crumbs. Shallow-fry the prawns, about four at a time, until golden brown and cooked through (about 3 minutes), turning once. Drain on absorbent paper and keep warm while the remainder are cooked. Serve hot.

\* *Peeled prawns with tail fin intact, cut open down the centre back, de-veined and pressed out flat.*

*Stuff each prawn with crab mixture*

*Dip prawns in beaten egg whites and coat with crumbs*

# Honey Nut Pastries
### *Plakoundes*

MAKES 18

**6 sheets Filo pastry**
**75 g (2½ oz) butter**
**60 g (2 oz) sugar**
**⅓ cup water**
**2 teaspoons honey**
**1½ teaspoons lemon juice**
**1 small strip lemon rind (peel)**
**clarified butter for frying**

**Filling**
**125 g (4 oz) coarsely ground almonds**
**1 egg yolk**
**30 g (1 oz) caster (powdered) sugar**
**¾ teaspoon ground cinnamon**
**¼ teaspoon grated nutmeg**

Thaw the pastry, if frozen, and keep wrapped in a kitchen towel until needed. Melt the butter and set aside.

Boil the sugar, water, honey and lemon juice together for 2 minutes. Add the lemon rind and continue to boil until syrupy (a further 5 to 6 minutes), then set aside to cool.

Mix the filling ingredients together. Cut the pastry sheets lengthways into three even-sized strips. Brush lightly with the melted butter and fold each in half to give pieces about 20 × 10 cm (8 × 4 in). Brush one side with more butter and place a spoonful of the filling towards one end. Fold the two sides in about 2 cm (¾ in) and fold the bottom over the filling. Then roll up tightly, brushing a little more butter on the end flap before pressing into place.

When all the pastries are rolled, heat about 2.5 cm (1 in) of clarified butter in the wok to moderate. Fry the pastries, about six at a time, until golden. Place in the pan with the end flaps downwards at first to prevent them unrolling during cooking. Turn carefully using two large spoons.

When they're golden on both sides, drain well on kitchen paper and arrange on a plate. Pour on the syrup and leave to cool before serving.

*Cut pastry into strips, keep remainder covered*

*Fill pastries and roll up tightly*

# Strawberry Cream Puffs

MAKES 36

**60 g (2 oz) butter**
**1¼ cups (10 fl oz) milk**
**1 lemon**
**2 teaspoons sugar**
**¼ teaspoon salt**
**1 cup (4 oz) flour**
**4 large eggs**
**1 cup (8 fl oz) whipped cream**
**1 punnet fresh strawberries (approx. 200 g/6½ oz)**

Place the butter in a saucepan and melt gently without allowing it to bubble. Add the milk and the grated rind (peel) of the lemon, and bring to the boil; simmer for 3 minutes. Add the sugar and salt and then quickly work in the flour, stirring with a wooden spoon; cook, stirring constantly, over moderate heat for about 5 minutes. Remove from the heat and beat in the eggs one at a time. Make sure each egg is fully incorporated into the mixture before you add the next one. The dough should be smooth and shiny.

Heat about 5 cm (2 in) clean cooking oil in the wok to moderate. Drop in teaspoonfuls of the mixture and fry for 4 to 6 minutes until golden and puffed, turning several times during cooking. The oil must not be allowed to overheat or the pastries would cook on the outside while the inside would remain sticky and undercooked. Drain the cooked cream puffs and allow to cool.

When cool, slit on one side with a sharp knife. Fill each with whipped cream and add half a strawberry to each, allowing the point of the berry to protrude from the slit. Dust with icing (confectioners') sugar and serve.

*Beat eggs, one at a time into cooked dough*

*Drop teaspoonfuls of mixture into hot oil*

# Pineapple Fritters

SERVES 6

**1 medium-sized fresh pineapple**
**½ cup (2 oz) flour**
**¼ cup (1 oz) chopped almonds**
**½ cup (4 fl oz) water**
**pinch of salt**
**1 tablespoon sugar**
**1 teaspoon baking powder**
**2 egg whites**

Peel the pineapple and cut into six thick slices. Place on a double thickness of kitchen paper and cover with more paper. Leave to absorb as much of the juice as possible.

Sift the flour into a mixing bowl and add the almonds, water, salt, sugar and baking powder. Beat until smooth.

Heat about 4 cm (1½ in) clarified butter or clean cooking oil in the wok to moderately hot. Beat the egg whites to soft peaks, then fold them into the batter. Dip the pineapple into the batter and place in the oil. Fry two or three pieces at a time until golden brown. Lift out and drain well on kitchen paper. Keep cooked fritters warm in a low oven with the door ajar.

Sprinkle with icing (confectioners') sugar and serve hot with vanilla ice-cream or whipped cream.

Thick slices of apple, cored but unpeeled, can be used instead of the pineapple. Or try ripe but firm bananas, halved lengthways.

*Peel pineapple and cut into thick slices*

*Press slices with paper towel to absorb juice*

# Poaching

Poaching is a simple, effective cooking technique which is largely overlooked in the home kitchen. It is the gentle cooking of foods in a liquid which remains at a temperature just below the boil. This is variously described as 'trembling', 'shivering' or 'barely simmering'. The objective is to cook gently and slowly so that the food retains its natural composition and shape, becomes well flavoured with the liquid in which it is being cooked, and retains all of its own natural moisture.

Poaching is employed in particular for foods of a delicate texture, such as fish and other seafood, poultry, the soft offal (brains and sweetbreads), firm fresh fruits and certain vegetables.

The stock used for poaching varies according to the dish and the seasonings added. It may be a classic *court bouillon* using diced vegetables, herbs and seasonings in a stock of dry white wine and water, a simple chicken or veal stock, a flavoured wine, or simply water enhanced with spices, citrus juices, sugar and liqueurs. The well-flavoured poaching liquor is often served with the dish as a sauce or a soup. It may be re-used in certain cases, for preparing another similar dish.

The large capacity of the wok, with its sloped sides, makes it an excellent poaching pan for foods as small as a pair of quails or a particularly excellent peach, or as large as a whole fish or joint of meat.

Although it differs in shape from the traditional elongated oval-shaped fish kettle, the wok serves this purpose well. Fish kettles are fitted with an internal basket which can be removed from the kettle and which prevents the tender fish breaking up after it is cooked. In the wok, the fish can rest on a perforated metal or wire mesh rack which will hold it above the centre bottom of the wok to prevent the possibility of spot-burning. It can be slipped out of the wok with fish intact after cooking. Chickens, ducks and small birds such as quails can also be poached on a rack or in a frying basket to make it easier to remove the tender cooked dish from the wok.

Generally the poaching liquor will be prepared in advance and simmered for some time to extract the full flavour from its ingredients. It is then strained into the wok and heated before the food is added.

When meats are being poached to render them tender, as in the case of brains or sweetbreads, or salt pork, they will be placed in the wok and covered with cold water, brought to poaching temperature and then left to cook gently until ready. This liquid is not retained for use as a soup or sauce.

Firm fresh fruit such as peaches, pears and plums can be transformed into exotic desserts by simply poaching in flavoured liquor, usually a combination of wine and sugar. The cooking liquor will thicken and caramelise during the cooking and is served with the fruit. If necessary, a thin sauce may be thickened slightly by the addition of a mixture of cornflour and cold water.

Dried fruits may be poached as well, either in water with sugar added to sweeten, or in sweetened wine or liqueurs. A handful of dried prunes, apricots and figs poached with water and a can of cherries (Hot Fruit Compote) makes a quick, delicious and health-giving dessert.

# Thai Prawns in Chilli and Lime Soup

**Tom Yam Kung**

SERVES 6

This is most impressive cooked at the table in a Chinese steamboat or a fondue pot.

**750 g (1½ lb) green prawns (raw shrimp), in the shell**
**6 cups (1½ litres) fish stock**
**1 lime, quartered**
**4 lime leaves**
**2 stalks lemon grass, sliced in halves**
**2 cloves garlic, sliced**
**2 fresh red chillies, sliced**
**1 tablespoon fish sauce (nam pla)\***
**1 teaspoon chilli sauce (optional)**
**salt and black pepper**
**4–6 shallots (scallions/spring onions)**
**additional lime juice**

Wash the prawns in cold water. Do not remove the shells. If desired, slit down the centre backs to remove the dark vein.

Bring the fish stock to a gentle boil. Add the lime, lime leaves, lemon grass (white root end only), garlic and chillies, and simmer for 10 to 12 minutes. Add the fish sauce, chilli sauce, salt and pepper to taste, and simmer for a further 10 to 12 minutes.

The prawns should be added about 7 minutes before serving time and gently poached in the piquant stock. Add the shallots, finely chopped, and extra lime juice to taste just before serving.

\* *A product from Thailand or Vietnam. If unobtainable use light soy sauce.*

*Add lime, leaves, chilli and lemon grass to stock*

*Add prawns to the well-flavoured stock*

# Mussels in Wine

**Moules Marinière**

SERVES 6

Mussel enthusiasts shun the use of the spoon and use instead one of the mussel shells to scoop up the delicious wine and cream-based soup in which these mussels are cooked and served. A bib is recommended.

**1¾ kg (3½ lb) fresh mussels**
**2 shallots (spring onions/scallions), chopped**
**½ stick celery (chopped)**
**1 tablespoon chopped parsley**
**2 cups (16 fl oz) dry white wine**
**1 cup (8 fl oz) water**
**1 bouquet garni (bunch of fresh herbs)**
**¼ teaspoon ground black pepper**
**pinch of salt**
**2 tablespoons thickened (heavy) cream**
**2 teaspoons butter**
**2 teaspoons flour**

Thoroughly wash the mussels, scrubbing the shells with a hard brush to remove any barnacles. Pull away the beards. Rinse in clean cold water.

Place the shallots and celery in the wok with half the parsley, and the wine, water, herbs, pepper and salt. Bring to the boil and boil briskly for 2 to 3 minutes.

Add the mussels, cover and cook for about 8 minutes until the mussels open. Shake the pan from time to time. Discard any mussels that do not open. Remove the mussels to a deep serving dish using a slotted spoon.

Return the liquid to the boil and discard the herbs. Mix the cream with the flour and butter, working to a smooth thin paste; pour into the wok and whisk until well blended. Add the remaining parsley and check for salt. Pour over the mussels and serve at once.

*Scrub mussels and pull away the beards*

*Mussels open when cooked*

# Duck Poached with Lemons and Limes

SERVES 6-8 AS AN APPETIZER

It may also be served to 4 to 6 people as a main course with other Chinese dishes.

**1 × 1.5 kg (3 lb) duck**
**1 lemon**
**1 lime**
**1 large shallot (scallion/spring onion), trimmed**
**3 thin slices fresh (root) ginger**
**1½ teaspoons salt**

Cut the duck into serving pieces and place in the wok. Quarter the lemon and lime without peeling, and arrange around the duck. Add the whole shallot and the ginger slices, the salt and water to cover. Cover the wok and bring the water just to the boil, then reduce heat and simmer with the water just barely trembling for about 1¾ hours until the duck is very tender.

Skim the fat from the surface and serve the duck in its soup, or serve meat and soup separately as preferred.

*Using poultry shears cut duck into serving pieces.*

*Place duck in wok and simmer with fruit*

# Veal with Tunafish Sauce
## Vitello Tonnato

SERVES 6–8

1 kg (2 lb) veal roast
   (topside, rump
   or shoulder)
2 fillets of anchovy
1 medium onion
2 cloves
1 bay leaf
1 stick celery
1 medium carrot
2 to 3 sprigs parsley
1½ teaspoons salt

**Sauce**
1 220 g (7 oz) can tuna,
   drained
2 fillets of anchovy
150 ml (5 fl oz) olive oil
1 to 2 lemons
1 tablespoon capers,
   drained

*Pierce veal and insert pieces of anchovy*

*Tie meat securely with string*

*Very slowly add oil to the tuna mixture until sauce is smooth and thick*

Pierce the veal with the point of a knife at intervals and insert small pieces of anchovy. Season the meat with salt and pepper. Roll it up, tie securely with string, and place in the wok. Peel the onion, and stud it all over with the cloves. Add it and the remaining ingredients to the wok. Add warm water to cover the meat, cover the wok and bring to the boil, then reduce the heat and leave to simmer gently for about 1½ hours.

Remove the meat from the wok and leave to cool, covered with a clean cloth.

Place the tuna in a food processor or blender with the anchovy and then gradually add the olive oil, blending at moderate speed until the oil has all been incorporated and the sauce is smooth and thick. Squeeze the lemons for juice and add to the sauce to taste. Add the capers, whole or finely chopped.

Untie the veal and slice thinly. Arrange overlapped on a serving plate. Pour on the sauce and garnish with twists of lemon.

This dish is even more delicious if it is prepared about 6 hours in advance to allow time for the flavours of the sauce to penetrate the meat.

# Chicken in Soy Sauce

*Place chicken on rack or chopsticks in wok*

*Add star anise, shallot and ginger*

*Pour in soy sauce, cover and simmer*

SERVES 4–6

**1 × 1.2 kg (2½ lb) roasting chicken**
**5 shallots (spring onions/scallions), trimmed**
**5 thick slices fresh (root) ginger**
**1 teaspoon sesame oil (optional)**
**2 Chinese star anise**

**Sauce**
**2 cups (16 fl oz) chicken stock or water**
**1 cup (8 fl oz) light soy sauce**
**½ cup (4 fl oz) dark soy sauce (mushroom soy)**
**½ cup (4 oz) sugar**

Clean the chicken and wipe with kitchen paper. Into the cavity put 2 shallots and 2 slices of ginger. Rub the skin with the sesame oil, if used. Place the chicken in the wok on a small oiled rack to hold it just above the bottom of the wok. Place the star anise and remaining shallots and ginger in the wok on either side of the chicken.

Add the sauce ingredients and bring to a gentle boil. Cover the wok, reduce the heat and simmer slowly with the bubbles just occasionally breaking the surface, until the chicken is completely tender (about 50 minutes). Turn once to ensure even cooking.

Lift the chicken out of the stock with two slotted spoons and drain thoroughly. Cut into serving pieces and serve hot with a little of the poaching liquid as a sauce.

The remaining liquid can be re-used for another chicken. A sliced fresh red chilli and a piece of orange or mandarin (tangerine) peel can be added to the poaching liquid for added flavour.

# Poached Whole Fish

*Add fish to court bouillon in wok*

*Sauté mushrooms until softened*

*Scrape skin away from cooked fish*

SERVES 4

**1 × 1 kg (2 lb) fresh fish (snapper, bream, porgy or sea bass)**

**Court Bouillon**
**4 cups (1 litre) water**
**1½ cups (12 fl oz) dry white wine**
**1½ teaspoons salt**
**1 medium onion, sliced**
**⅓ stick celery, sliced**
**1 medium carrot, sliced**
**1 clove garlic, lightly crushed**
**5 black peppercorns**
**1 clove**
**1 bay leaf**
**½ lemon rind**
**1 sprig each fresh fennel, thyme and parsley**

**Tomato and Mushroom Sauce**
**125 g (4 oz) fresh button mushrooms, sliced**
**75 g (2½ oz) butter**
**1 tablespoon flour**
**2 egg yolks**
**2 tablespoons thickened (heavy) cream**
**1 teaspoon tomato paste, purée or powder**

Clean and scale the fish and wash in cold water. Set aside.

Place the ingredients for the court bouillon in the wok and bring to the boil. Cover and simmer for 25 minutes.

Add the fish, reduce the heat, and allow the fish to simmer very gently with the liquid just barely trembling, for about 20 minutes.

Lift out the fish using two egg slices (egg lifters), transfer it to a warmed serving dish, cover and keep warm. Retain the court bouillon.

Sauté the mushrooms in half the butter until softened. Remove from the wok. Add the remaining butter and the flour, and cook, stirring, on moderate heat until it is lightly coloured. Add about 1½ cups (12 fl oz) of the retained stock and bring to the boil; stir on moderate heat until thickened. Remove from the heat and stir in the egg yolks and the cream and tomato paste. Beat for 1 minute, then add the mushrooms and heat through.

Carefully scrape the skin from the fish and mask the fish with the sauce. Serve at once.

Poached fish is also delicious served cold and is an ideal dish for a light lunch or on a cold buffet table. After scraping away the skin, mask the fish with a thin coating of mayonnaise and decorate it with narrow strips of red and green capsicum (bell pepper) and rolled anchovies or strips of black olive.

# Sole Véronique

SERVES 6

This light and creamy fish dish can also be served as an appetizer or second (fish) course. Presented on a bed of white or saffron rice, it should serve 8 to 10.

**750 g (1½ lb) fillets of sole or other small fish fillets**
**1 cup (8 fl oz) water**
**¾ cup (6 fl oz) dry white wine**
**6 black peppercorns**
**1 large shallot (spring onion/scallion), trimmed**
**155 g (5 oz) seedless green grapes**
**lemon juice**

**Sauce**
**1 tablespoon butter**
**2 tablespoons flour**
**⅓ cup milk**
**2–3 tablespoons thickened (heavy) cream**
**2 egg yolks, beaten**

Wash the fillets and dry on kitchen paper. Fold each piece in half and arrange in a well-buttered dish that will fit inside the wok. Add the water, wine, peppercorns and shallot, and cover the dish with a piece of buttered paper. Set on a rack in the wok, add water to the level of the rack and cover. Bring the water to the boil and steam the fish over moderately high heat for about 12 minutes.

When done, transfer the fish to a warmed serving plate. Cover with foil and keep it warm in a low oven with the door ajar while you make the sauce. Reserve 1¼ cups (10 fl oz) of the poaching liquor.

Peel the grapes and cut into halves. Sprinkle with a little lemon juice and set aside.

Melt the butter in a clean wok and add the flour. Cook briefly, then pour in the milk and the reserved stock. Stir until the sauce boils and thickens slightly (about 2 minutes), then remove from the heat. Mix the cream and egg yolks together and add to the sauce. Beat until smooth, then return to low heat to cook until the sauce is thick and creamy. Stir continually to prevent burning or curdling.

Add the grapes, then pour the sauce over the fish.

Cover fish with buttered paper

Peel and halve grapes, remove seeds

# Pears in Red Wine

SERVES 6

**6 ripe but firm pears**
**½ cup (4 oz) sugar**
**1½ cups (12 fl oz) red wine**
**1½ cups (12 fl oz) water**
**1 tablespoon vanillin sugar***
**1 tablespoon cornflour (cornstarch)**

Peel the pears and set aside. Mix the sugar, wine and water together in the wok and bring to the boil, stirring until the sugar is dissolved.

Add the pears and vanillin sugar and reduce the heat. Partially cover the wok and gently poach the pears for about 1¼ hours until they are very tender but still holding their shape. The syrup should be reduced to about 1¼ cups.

Use a slotted spoon to lift the pears from the wok and transfer to glass dessert dishes.

Mix the cornflour with an equal amount of cold water and slowly stir into the syrup. Stir on moderate heat until the sauce is thick and transparent. Spoon over the pears. Serve hot with whipped cream.

\* *Finely ground sugar impregnated with the flavour of vanilla —by storing a vanilla pod in a jar of caster (powdered) sugar. If unobtainable, substitute 1 teaspoon of vanilla essence.*

*Add pears to wine syrup in wok*

*Lift cooked pears out of syrup with a slotted spoon*

*Vanilla beans give a superb flavour to sugar*

# Apricot Delight
## Mishmisheya

SERVES 6

The smooth purée of dried apricots highlighted by the crunchy texture of almonds and the hint of orange-flavoured liqueur is typical of the extravagant sweet dishes from the Middle East. Sour cream can be served as the accompaniment for those who prefer a less rich dessert.

**375 g (12 oz) dried apricots**
**125 g (4 oz) sugar**
**90 g (3 oz) blanched almonds**
**1 cup (8 oz) thickened (heavy) cream**
**2 tablespoons caster (powdered) sugar**
**1 tablespopon Cointreau or Grand Marnier**
**1½ tablespoons toasted chopped almonds**

Wash the apricots and place in the wok with water to cover. Bring almost to the boil and poach gently for 30 minutes.

Add the sugar and stir until dissolved, then remove from the heat and allow to cool slightly.

Transfer to a blender or food processor and grind to a smooth purée. Stir in the blanched almonds which have been cut into slivers, then chill thoroughly.

Whip the cream, adding the sugar and liqueur. Spoon the apricot purée into a glass serving dish and top with the whipped cream and the toasted almonds.

*Add sugar to poached dried apricots in wok*

*Purée the poached dried apricots*

*Stir in the slivered almonds*

# Floating Islands in Blackberry Sauce

SERVES 4

**1 450 g (14 oz) can blackberries**
**½ teaspoon salt**
**2 egg whites**
**1 tablespoon caster (powdered) sugar**

Pour the blackberries and their liquid into a blender and purée, then pass through a fine nylon sieve to remove the seeds. Heat gently and set aside.

Bring about 5 cups of water to a gentle boil in the wok and add the salt.

Beat the egg whites until firm, add the sugar and continue to beat until it stands in firm peaks and is very shiny. Take tablespoons of the mixture and drop into the water. Poach, about six at a time, for 4 to 5 minutes on one side, then flip over and cook on the other side for the same time. Remove the meringues with a slotted spoon.

Reheat the berry purée gently, then pour into a wide shallow serving dish. Float the meringues on top. Serve as soon as the last batch are cooked.

Lightly sweetened cream can accompany this light and tangy dessert.

*Sieve the puréed black-berries to remove seeds*

*Beat egg whites and sugar until they stand in peaks*

*Drop meringue into water and poach*

# Hot Fruit Compote

SERVES 6

**75 g (2½ oz) dried apricots**
**155 g (5 oz) dessert prunes**
**125 g (4 oz) dried figs**
**1 can 425 g (13½ oz) black cherries in syrup**
**2½ cups (20 fl oz) water**

Place the fruit and liquid from the cherries in the wok and add the water. Cover and bring almost to the boil, then poach gently for about 1½ hours until the fruit is tender and the liquid well reduced. The cherry liquor should provide enough sugar to sweeten the dish.

Serve hot in small glass dishes with a generous topping of whipped cream.

*Place fruit and cherry syrup in wok with water*

*Poach until fruit is tender*

# Prunes and Oranges in Port

SERVES 6–8

**375 g (12 oz) dessert prunes**
**2 large sweet oranges**
**5 cloves**
**1 cinnamon stick**
**¾ cup (6 fl oz) Port**
**2½ cups (20 fl oz) water**
**½ cup (4 oz) sugar**

Wash the prunes and soak for 2 hours, then drain well.

Use a sharp knife to thickly peel the oranges, ensuring that all pith is removed. Separate each segment of orange, cutting away all membranes. Reserve a strip of the rind (peel) for use in the dish, and scrape away its pith.

Place the prunes, oranges and reserved orange rind in the wok with the remaining ingredients. Cover and poach gently until the prunes are tender. Serve hot or cold with fresh or whipped cream.

*Peel all skin and pith from oranges*

*Separate oranges into segments*

*Add port to fruit, sugar and spices*

# *Steaming*

Steaming as a cooking method was discovered by the Chinese many centuries ago. Chefs, regarding the applying of fire directly to foods as a barbarian practice, sought various methods to introduce an intermediary between food and the cooking pot. Frying and sautéeing became popular, but it was the purity of steaming that had the most appeal.

Not that steaming remained the exclusive right of Chinese cooks. For centuries the British have relied on steaming for their delicious puddings, both sweet and savoury. And as health-consciousness increasingly influences cooking styles around the world, cooks are turning to steaming as a simple and unrivalled way to prepare light, low-calorie and delicious meals.

Steam is no more than the result of the meeting of those two old antagonists, fire and water. But steam is hotter than water can ever be—once water has reached the boil at 100°C (212°F), it requires additional heat before it can vaporise into steam. The steam quickly permeates whatever is being cooked, keeping the moisture in. Therefore steam cooks more thoroughly and rapidly than any other technique. It saves time, and time means money when gas, electricity or other valuable fuels are being used. The problems of burning and overcooking are virtually eliminated with steaming, and as a method of reheating food, steaming is invaluable.

The wok is an ideal steaming vessel. The various bamboo, metal or wire racks made to accompany the wok, are designed to fit into its curved bottom allowing space below for the water. The food to be cooked is placed in a dish on this rack and the wok lid set in place above. This fits snugly inside the rim of the wok. Steaming baskets of various sizes are also used with the wok. Smaller ones stand on a rack inside the wok and are covered with the lid, while larger ones sit directly inside the rim of the wok and their own lids are used to cover. These are used particularly for the many snack-like dishes of which the Chinese are specialists, but they are now being put to good use in the cooking of a variety of dishes.

For successful steaming, ensure that the wok sits firmly over the heat source— in this instance gas or electricity are equally effective. Choose a rack which allows about 5 cm (2 in) of space beneath and add water to the level of the rack. Place the food in a dish with sides high enough to contain the cooking liquids plus the quantity of extra liquid which will be added to the pan through the process of condensation during the cooking—the steam will condense on the inside of the lid and drop in to the dish. The wok lid should fit snugly inside the rim of the wok. To prevent leakage, place a twisted dish towel around the edge of the lid making sure that no parts come in contact with the heat source.

The water should be brought to a rapid boil, then the heat regulated in accordance with the needs of the particular dish, i.e. high, moderate, gentle, etc. as explained in each recipe. All that needs to be done through the cooking is to ensure that the water level does not drop much below the level of the rack.

A warning note: steam, as we've already mentioned, is very hot. Wear a pair of thick oven gloves or protect the hands with a cloth when removing a dish from a steamer. And always lift the back of the lid first to direct the cloud of released steam away from hands and face.

# Scallop Mousseline in Saffron Sauce

SERVES 6

**500 g (1 lb) fresh scallops**
**2 teaspoons lemon juice**
**2 eggs**
**1 tablespoon flour**
**2 teaspoons cornflour (cornstarch)**
**2 tablespoons fish stock or water**
**1 fish stock cube crumbled**
**salt and pepper**
**1 shallot (spring onion/scallion), chopped**

**Saffron Sauce**
**½ cup (4 fl oz) milk**
**¼ teaspoon saffron powder**
**¼ teaspoon mustard powder**
**⅓ teaspoon salt**
**1 tablespoon butter**
**2½ teaspoons flour**
**½ cup (4 fl oz) thin (light) cream**
**2 egg yolks**

Marinate the scallops in the lemon juice for 10 minutes. Transfer to a food processor or blender, and purée to a smooth paste. Add the remaining ingredients and purée again until smooth. Pour into six buttered heatproof dishes and cover each with a piece of buttered aluminium foil.

Set on a rack in the wok and add water to the level of the rack. Bring to the boil, then steam gently for about 25 minutes until set.

Turn on to medium-sized plates and coat with the sauce. Garnish each plate with a cooked prawn (shrimp) or poached scallop with the roe attached, and a sprig of coriander.

To make the Saffron Sauce, scald the milk in a small saucepan with the saffron, mustard and salt. Remove from the heat and set aside.

Melt the butter in another pan. Add the flour and cook, stirring for 1 minute. Pour in the milk and bring to the boil, stirring; simmer for 2 minutes, then remove from the heat.

Beat the cream and egg yolks together, and pour into the pan. Beat until the sauce is smooth, then return to low heat and cook gently until the sauce thickens (about 3 minutes), stirring constantly.

*Pour the puréed scallop mixture into dishes*

*Cover dishes with foil and place on a rack in the wok*

*Carefully turn out the cooked mousseline*

# Steamed Stuffed King Prawns

SERVES 6 AS AN APPETIZER, 4 AS A MAIN COURSE

**12 green king prawns (large raw shrimp), in the shell**

**Seasoning**
**½ teaspoon salt**
**½ teaspoon sugar**
**¼ teaspoon white pepper**
**½ teaspoon sesame oil (optional)**
**2 teaspoons light soy sauce**
**1 tablespoon finely chopped shallots (spring onions/scallions)**
**2 teaspoons grated fresh (root) ginger**

Wash the prawns and use a sharp knife to cut through the shells along the backs; pick out the intestinal veins and rinse the prawns in cold water. Mix the remaining ingredients together and insert a little into the cut section of each prawn.

Place the prawns on an oiled plate and set on a rack in the wok. Cover tightly and steam briskly for 8 minutes. Serve with steamed rice.

*Cut prawns along the back and remove the vein*

*Insert seasonings into each cut section*

# Egg Custard with Shrimps

SERVES 4

**250 g (8 oz) peeled raw shrimp (small green prawns)**
**½ teaspoon salt**
**1 tablespoon dry sherry or ginger wine**
**1 teaspoon finely chopped ginger**
**6 large eggs**
**1 large shallot (spring onion/scallion), finely chopped**
**¾ teaspoon salt**
**pinch of pepper**

Wash the shrimp and drain well. Place in a dish and season with the ½ teaspoon of salt, the sherry and ginger and leave for 10 minutes, then pour off the excess liquid.

Lightly beat the eggs, adding the shallot, salt and pepper. Divide the shrimp between four heatproof covered dishes and pour the egg mixture on top.

Set on a rack in the wok and steam over gently boiling water for 12 minutes, or until firm. Do not overcook.

*Pour the egg mixture into heatproof bowls on top of the shrimps*

*Cover with foil and steam in a basket or on a rack in the wok*

# Stuffed Vine Leaves
## *Dolmades*

MAKES 48

**1 × 200 g (6½ oz) pack of vine leaves in brine**
**125 g (4 oz) minced (ground) beef**
**1 medium onion, chopped**
**2 cloves garlic, chopped**
**3 large tomatoes**
**2 tablespoons chopped parsley**
**2 tablespoons chopped celery leaves**
**2 tablespoons chopped almonds**
**1¼ cups (6 oz) raw long-grain rice**
**1 cup (8 fl oz) tomato juice**
**2 tablespoons olive oil**

Drain the vine leaves, cover with boiling water and leave for 20 minutes. Drain, rinse in another lot of boiling water, and cover with cold water until needed.

Sauté the beef, onion and garlic lightly in a little of the olive oil. Finely chop 1 tomato and add to the pan along with the parsley, celery and almonds. Sauté briefly, mixing well.

Cover the rice with boiling water and leave to stand for 1 minute, then drain thoroughly and add to the meat mixture.

Drain the vine leaves and fill each with a teaspoon of the mixture, placing it on the ribbed side of the leaves.

Fold over the stem section first, then the two sides and roll up towards the pointed end of the leaf. Arrange closely together in a lightly oiled dish. Pour on the tomato juice and the olive oil. Slice the remaining tomatoes and place over the vine leaf rolls. Top with any remaining vine leaves.

Set on a rack in the wok, add water to the level of the rack, cover the wok and steam for about 1¼ hours until the rice has expanded and become tender. Check the level of the water every 15 minutes and top up as necessary. It may be necessary to add a little more tomato juice during cooking as it becomes absorbed.

Serve the Dolmades warm or cold, with a dressing of olive oil and plain yoghurt or sour cream.

*Drain vine leaves and cover with boiling water*

*Add soaked and drained rice to sautéed beef*

*Place the filling on ribbed side of leaves*

*Roll up and place on an oiled plate, then steam*

# Cabbage Rolls

**MAKES 12**

1 × 1½ kg (3 lb) cabbage
375 g (12 oz) coarsely
 minced (ground) pork
1 large onion, chopped
1 large tomato, chopped
2 tablespoons butter
1½ tablespoons flour
1½ teaspoons sweet
 paprika
salt and black pepper
2 teaspoons chopped
 parsley
¼ teaspoon dried oregano
1 egg, beaten

**Tomato Sauce**
1 medium onion, finely
 chopped
1 large tomato, chopped
1 clove garlic, crushed
1 tablespoon butter
½ teaspoon sugar
salt and black pepper
½ cup (4 fl oz) thickened
 (heavy) cream

Separate the cabbage leaves and select 12 large ones for the rolls. Trim away the central stems. Place the leaves and about 125 g (4 oz) of the remaining cabbage in the wok. Cover with boiling water and simmer gently for about 5 minutes until the leaves have softened. Drain well.

Wipe out the wok, then fry the pork, onion and tomato in the butter for about 5 minutes, stirring frequently. Add the flour and paprika, salt and pepper to taste, and the herbs. Cover and simmer gently for 5 to 6 minutes. Remove from the heat and leave to cool for about 10 minutes.

Stir the egg into the pork mixture. Chop the blanched excess cabbage finely, squeeze to remove as much water as possible, and mix into the pork mixture.

Divide the filling between the 12 prepared leaves and roll up each to enclose the filling. Place in a dish, seams downwards, and set on a rack in a clean wok. Add water to the level of the rack and steam, tightly covered, for about 45 minutes. Add more water as needed.

In a separate saucepan or wok, prepare the sauce by sautéeing the onion, tomato and garlic in the butter until soft. Add the sugar, salt and pepper to taste, and simmer gently until thick. Stir in the cream just before using.

To serve the cabbage rolls, drain and arrange on a plate. Pour on the sauce.

*Cover cabbage with boiling water, then cook*

*Divide filling among leaves and roll up*

*Cover and steam in a dish on rack in wok*

# Cucumber with Pork Stuffing

SERVES 6

1 large cucumber
185 g (6 oz) lean pork, finely minced (ground)
1 large shallot (spring onion/scallion), chopped
2 slices fresh (root) ginger, chopped
2 teaspoons light soy sauce
¾ teaspoon dry sherry
¾ teaspoon sugar
1 teaspoon cornflour (cornstarch)

Sauce
2 teaspoons light soy sauce
2 teaspoons Chinese oyster sauce
1 teaspoon cornflour (cornstarch)

Wipe the cucumber and remove the ends, then cut into six thick slices. Use a small knife to remove the seed core, making each piece of cucumber into a ring.

Mix the pork with the remaining ingredients and use to fill the cucumber rings. Set on a lightly oiled plate. Place the plate on a rack in the wok and add water to just below the rack. Cover and steam gently for about 25 minutes.

Drain the liquid from the plate into a clean wok and add the other sauce ingredients. Bring to the boil and stir for about 1 minute, then pour over the cucumbers and serve.

*Cut cucumber into thick slices and remove seeds*

*Fill cucumber with meat mixture, set on plate*

# Pork Dumplings
## Siew Mai

MAKES 18

280 g (9 oz) fatty pork
2 dried Chinese mushrooms, soaked
1 shallot (spring onion/scallion), chopped
½ teaspoon grated fresh (root) ginger
2 teaspoons chopped parsley
½ egg white, beaten
¾ teaspoon salt
1 teaspoon sugar
1½ teaspoons light soy sauce
½ teaspoon dark soy sauce (mushroom soy)
1 tablespoon cornflour (cornstarch)
2–3 tablespoons green peas
1 small carrot
18 fresh or frozen wonton wrappers

Cut the pork into small pieces and place in a food processor or blender. Mince (grind) to a smooth paste then transfer to a dish. Squeeze the water from the mushrooms, remove stems and chop the caps finely. Mix the ingredients, except peas, carrot and wrappers, together with the pork, kneading until thoroughly mixed and a sticky paste. Cover with plastic wrap and chill for 1 hour.

Parboil the peas and the carrot which has been cut into very small dice. Drain and set aside.

Thaw and separate the wrappers, trim off the four corners, then cover with a cloth until needed.

To form the dumplings, place 2 teaspoonfuls of the mixture in the centre of each wrapper and pleat the wrapper up and around the sides. Press it firmly on to the filling leaving the top open. Place 2 peas and a cube of carrot on the top of each dumpling and press lightly into the filling.

Set the dumplings into a lightly greased steaming basket or on an oiled wire cake cooler, and set on a rack in the wok.

Add water to below the level of the rack to prevent the boiling water touching the dumplings. Cover, bring to the boil and steam for about 12 minutes until cooked through. Serve straight from the steamer with dips of hot mustard and soy sauce.

*Remove stems from soaked and squeezed mushrooms and chop caps finely*

*Press wrapping firmly around filling to form a dumpling*

# Chinese Pork Buns
## *Cha Siew Pow*

MAKES 12

**Dough**
2¼ cups (9 oz) flour
1 tablespoon baking powder
⅓ cup (3 oz) sugar
1 tablespoon softened lard
⅔ cup (5 fl oz) lukewarm water

**Filling**
125 g (4 oz) Chinese roast pork,
1 large shallot (spring onion/scallion), chopped
2 teaspoons light soy sauce
1 teaspoon dark soy sauce (mushroom soy)
1½ teaspoons Hoisin sauce (sweet bean paste)
1 teaspoon Chinese oyster sauce
1 tablespoon sugar
1 teaspoon dry sherry
⅓ cup (2½ fl oz) water
1 tablespoon cornflour (cornstarch)

Sift the flour and baking powder into a mixing bowl. Add the sugar and mix well, then add the lard and water, mixing to a soft dough. Knead lightly until smooth. Cover with plastic wrap and leave for about 30 minutes.

Thinly slice the pork and cut into small squares. Sauté the pork and shallot in about 1 tablespoon vegetable oil for 1 minute; then add the sauces, sugar and sherry and sauté for a further 1 minute. Mix the water and cornflour together, pour in and sauté, stirring, until thickened. Transfer to a plate to cool.

Roll the dough out into a long sausage shape and cut into 12 pieces. Flatten each with the fingers into a disc about 10 cm (4 in) across. Place a portion of filling in the centre and pull the dough up around the filling, pinching it together into a point. Cut a small square of greaseproof paper, dip into water and stick over the joint.

When all buns are prepared in this way, place them paper downwards in a steaming basket or on a rack. Set in the wok with the water level a good 5 cm (2 in) below the rack. Cover, and steam for about 12 minutes over rapidly boiling water until the buns have puffed out and are dry and springy to the touch. *Cha Siew Pow* must be served at once to be at their best.

*Flatten dough, add filling and pull dough over*

*Wet greaseproof paper and place over join*

## New Potatoes with Julienne Vegetables

SERVES 4–6

12 small new potatoes (approx. 500 g/1 lb)
1 medium carrot
1 medium zucchini (courgette)
1 stick celery
1 large shallot (spring onion/scallion)
2 sprigs fresh dill or fennel
²⁄₃ cup sour cream
1 tablespoon thickened (heavy) cream
salt

Thoroughly scrub the potatoes and prick in several places.
Place in a heatproof dish and set on a rack in the wok.
Add water to the level of the rack, cover and bring to the boil.
Steam for about 8 minutes.

In the meantime, peel the vegetables and cut into julienne
(matchstick) strips. Arrange over the potatoes with the herbs
on top. Return to the steamer and cook for a further
8 minutes or until the potatoes and julienne vegetables are
tender. Remove from the wok and drain liquid from the dish.

Mix the creams together and spoon over the vegetables or
serve separately.

## Choko (Chayote) with Parsley Butter

SERVES 4–6

2 medium chokoes (chayote/summer squash),
   or zucchini (courgette)
salt
1½ tablespoons butter
1 tablespoon finely chopped parsley

Peel the choko or other vegetable and cut into strips.
Place in a heatproof dish and sprinkle lightly with salt.
Set on a rack in the wok and steam over rapidly boiling
water for about 8 minutes, tightly covered.

Drain off any liquid that has accumulated in the dish,
add the butter cut into dice and the parsley. Return to the
steamer and cook for a further 1 to 2 minutes. Serve at once.

*Set potatoes on a heatproof dish in wok*

*Cut vegetables into julienne strips*

*Peel choko under water to prevent staining hands*

*Slice choko, then cut into strips*

## Broccoli Shape

SERVES 4–6

Try this recipe also for Brussels sprouts, asparagus or small new potatoes, adjusting the cooking time accordingly.

**2 large heads broccoli
    (approx. 375 g/12 oz)
2 teaspoons butter,
    cut into small dice
¾ teaspoon salt**

**Quick Hollandaise Sauce
6 egg yolks
1 tablespoon lemon juice
pinch of salt
250 g (8 oz) butter**

*Dot butter on broccoli flowerets*

Wash the broccoli thoroughly and cut into flowerets. Place in a dish with the flowers upwards and scatter the butter pieces and salt over the top. Set on a rack in the wok, add water to the level of the rack, cover and steam for about 15 minutes or until just tender. Do not overcook.

To make the Hollandaise Sauce, melt the butter until it just begins to bubble then remove quickly from the heat. Place the egg yolks, lemon juice and salt into a blender or food processor and blend until slightly thickened, then slowly drizzle in the butter, blending until all has been incorporated. Serve with the hot vegetables.

## Little Carrot Cups

SERVES 6

**410 g (13 oz) carrots
1 tablespoon lemon juice
2 tablespoons butter, softened
2 eggs
¾ teaspoon salt
¼ teaspoon sugar
1½ teaspoons finely chopped parsley, or 6 capers**

Peel the carrots, slice them and cook in boiling water without salt for 12 to 15 minutes until tender.

Drain the carrots well and transfer to a blender or food processor with the remaining ingredients, except parsley or capers. Blend to a smooth purée.

Butter six small heatproof dishes or cups, and sprinkle in the chopped parsley, or place a caper in the bottom of each. Pour in the carrot mixture and cover each with a piece of buttered aluminium foil.

Set on a rack in the wok and add water to just above the level of the rack. Cover and bring to the boil. Steam for about 18 minutes until set. Remove from the wok and leave to stand in the dishes for about 3 minutes before turning out to serve.

*Spoon puréed carrot mixture into dishes*

*Place in basket, cover and steam*

# Steak and Kidney Pudding

SERVES 6

**Pastry**
125 g (4 oz) grated fresh suet
2 cups (8 oz) flour
½ cup (1 oz) fresh (soft) breadcrumbs
½ teaspoon salt
¾ cup (6 fl oz) water

**Filling**
750 g (1½ lb) stewing steak
250 g (8 oz) ox kidneys
2 tablespoons seasoned flour
1 small onion
125 g (4 oz) fresh mushrooms
2 teaspoons Worcestershire sauce (optional)
2 teaspoons tomato paste, purée or powder
1¼ teaspoons salt
½ teaspoon ground black pepper
¾ cup (6 fl oz) beef stock

Place the suet in a mixing bowl and sift on the flour. Add the crumbs and salt and mix thoroughly. Pour in the water and work to a soft dough. Roll out on a floured board to about 0.5 cm (¼ in) thickness. Use about three-quarters of the dough to line a 1½ litre (6 cup) pudding basin, reserving the remainder for the top.

Cut the steak into cubes and place in a plastic or paper bag with the seasoned flour. Trim and cube the kidneys and add to the steak. Close the bag and shake vigorously to lightly and evenly coat the meat with the flour.

Finely chop the onion and slice the mushrooms. Place a layer of meat in the pudding basin and top with a thin layer of onion and mushrooms. Repeat layering until all the filling has been used up, ending with a layer of steak and kidney.

Mix the remaining ingredients together and pour carefully down the side of the pudding. The liquid should not be less than 2 cm (¾ in) from the top. Dampen the edges of the pastry with a wet finger or a pastry brush dipped in water. Cut the remaining pastry to fit the top, set in place and pinch the edges together to seal.

Cover the top with a piece of greased greaseproof paper and tie securely in position with string. Cover with a large square of clean pudding cloth (cheesecloth) and tie in the same way as the paper, then pull the corners of the cloth up over the top of the pudding and tie them together.

Set the pudding on a rack in the wok, add water to halfway up the sides of the pudding basin, cover and bring to the boil. Steam gently for about 5 hours, until the pastry has expanded and is light and dry to the touch, and the meat very tender. Remove from the wok and allow to cool for about 10 minutes before opening.

When the pudding is cut open, additional rich beef stock can be added before serving, as the gravy in the pudding will be very concentrated.

*Grate the fresh suet for the pastry*

*Roll pastry out and line bowl*

*Layer meat and vegetables in pastry-lined bowl*

*Top with remaining pastry, dampen edge*

# Baby Lamb with Herbs and Garlic

*Insert herbs and garlic in cuts in lamb*

*Place lamb in a dish in wok on rack, add water*

SERVES 4–6

Generous amounts of fresh herbs and garlic are used to flavour this dish, yet the result is a very subtle flavour and a delicious fragrance which complements the lamb perfectly.

**1¼ kg (2½ lb) leg of young lamb**
**6–8 sprigs fresh rosemary**
**6–8 sprigs fresh thyme**
**6–8 sprigs fresh sage or oregano**
**6 cloves garlic**
**1¼ teaspoons salt**
**½ teaspoon ground black pepper**

Trim the lamb and puncture at regular intervals with the point of a sharp knife. Insert the sprigs of herbs and the peeled whole cloves of garlic into the holes. Rub the lamb with the salt and pepper.

Place in a dish and set on a rack in the wok. Add water to the level of the rack, cover and steam over gently boiling water for about 1¾ hours, or until tender.

Drain well, carve at the table or slice the meat and arrange overlapped on a serving plate. Pour the liquid from the dish into a small jug to serve as the gravy.

# Pork Ribs in Black Bean and Chilli Sauce

SERVES 4

Serve this salty and hot dish with other *dim sum* dishes for
a Chinese-style breakfast or brunch; or as an appetizer;
or serve as a main course with other Chinese dishes.

4 pork spareribs\* or pork chops (approx. 500 g/1 lb)
2 shallots (spring onions/scallions), finely chopped
2 cloves garlic, finely chopped
2 slices fresh (root) ginger, finely chopped
2 teaspoons Chinese salted black beans, chopped
1 tablespoon light soy sauce
2 teaspoons dark soy sauce (mushroom soy)
2 teaspoons sugar
1 tablespoon dry sherry
½ teaspoon sesame oil (optional)
1 fresh red chilli

Cut the pork into bite-sized pieces and place in a heatproof
dish. Scatter the prepared ingredients and seasonings on top.
Finely shred or chop the chilli, discarding the seeds for a
milder taste; scatter on top of the pork.

Set the dish on a rack in the wok. Add water to the level
of the rack, cover and steam over gently boiling water for
about 1¾ hours, until the meat is very tender.

\* *The meaty fresh bacon ('five flowered pork') cut —
not trimmed rib bones (American spareribs).*

*Cut spareribs into bite-sized pieces*

*Scatter ingredients over*

# Lion's Head Meatballs

SERVES 4

750 g (1½ lb) boneless
    leg of pork
1 teaspoon salt
¼ teaspoon pepper
1 tablespoon light soy
    sauce
2 teaspoons dry sherry
1 teaspoon sugar
¾ teaspoon sesame oil
    (optional)
90 g (3 oz) canned water
    chestnuts, drained
1½ teaspoons finely
    chopped fresh (root)
    ginger
2 tablespoons chopped
    shallots (spring onions/
    scallions)
250 g (8 oz) Chinese
    cabbage (*bok choy*),
    or Tientsin cabbage
1 cup (8 fl oz) chicken
    stock

*Separate leaves and stalks of Tientsin cabbage*

*Wrap each meatball in cabbage leaves*

Cut the pork into cubes and place in a food processor fitted
with the chopping blade or in a mincer (grinder) and grind
to a slightly coarse paste. Mix in the seasoning ingredients.

Drain and chop the water chestnuts and mix with the pork,
adding the ginger and shallots. Mix well, using wet hands,
then form into four large meatballs. Wash the cabbage and
separate leaves and stalks. Wrap each meatball in one or
two cabbage leaves. Place the stalks in the bottom of a
heatproof dish and arrange the meatballs on top.
Cover with cabbage leaves, and pour in the stock.

Set the dish on a rack in the wok, add water to
level of the rack and bring to the boil. Cover and
steam for about 1 hour over rapidly boiling water.

# Steamed Ham

SERVES 8

**1 × 2 kg (4 lb) raw smoked ham (gammon)**
**1 tablespoon whole cloves**
**1 orange**
**1½ tablespoons clear honey**
**1 tablespoon Cointreau or Grand Marnier**
**3 slices brown or wholemeal (wholewheat) bread**

Cut away the skin of the ham leaving a thin layer of fat on the meat. Score through the fat in a criss-cross pattern and stud with the cloves. Place the ham in a dish and set on a rack in the wok. Add water to the level of the rack, cover and steam for about 2½ hours, until the ham is tender enough that the bone can be easily pulled out. Ensure that the water is topped up from time to time during cooking.

Remove the ham, de-bone, and discard the cloves. Squeeze the orange and mix the juice with the honey and liqueur in a small saucepan. Bring to the boil and simmer for about 2 minutes. Use a pastry brush to spread the syrup evenly over the ham. Reserve any remaining syrup to serve separately.

Toast the bread, then cut into pieces and place in a blender or food processor. Chop to reasonably fine crumbs. Grate the orange rind and mix with the crumbs. Press this mixture on to the ham, coating all surfaces.

Cut into thick slices and serve warm with the syrup.

*Remove skin from gammon (raw smoked ham) leaving thin layer of fat*

*Score ham and stud with whole cloves*

*Set ham on a rack, add water and steam for about 2½ hours until tender*

# Oriental-style Trout with Rosemary

SERVES 2

2 fresh trout (approx. 315 g/10 oz each)
1 teaspoon salt
2 teaspoons dry sherry
3 large fresh mushrooms
2 shallots (spring onions/scallions), shredded
5 slices fresh ginger, shredded
1 tablespoon light soy sauce
1½ tablespoons dry sherry
¾ teaspoon fresh rosemary, or ½ teaspoon
    dried rosemary, chopped
pinch of ground black pepper

Clean and wash the fish, leaving the heads and tails intact.
Score lightly three or four times on each side. Place on an
oval dish and sprinkle on the salt and 2 teaspoons of sherry
Set aside for 10 minutes.

Peel the mushrooms, remove stems and shred the caps.
Arrange the shredded mushrooms, shallots and ginger over
the fish. Pour excess salty liquid off the fish and set the plate
on a rack in the wok.

Add water to the level of the rack and bring to the boil.
Splash the soy sauce and sherry over the fish and scatter on
the rosemary and pepper. Cover tightly and steam for
9 minutes or until the meat can be easily lifted from the
bones. Serve at once on the same plate.

Score fish three to four times
on each side

Fish and vegetables are set on
a plate in wok

Scatter rosemary over fish
and steam, covered

# Scallops in Garlic Oyster Sauce

Steam scallops with wine and flavourings

Add cooked scallops to stir-fried vegetables

SERVES 4–6

750 g (1½ lb) fresh scallops
1 teaspoon crushed garlic
1 tablespoon ginger wine or dry sherry
155 g (5 oz) fresh bean sprouts
1 medium-sized red capsicum (bell pepper), or chilli
2 large shallots (spring onions/scallions)

**Sauce**
⅔ cup chicken stock
2 teaspoons dark soy sauce (mushroom soy)
2 teaspoons Chinese oyster sauce
2 teaspoons cornflour (cornstarch)
½ teaspoon sugar

Rinse the scallops and drain. Place in a dish and add half the garlic and the wine or sherry. Mix in lightly. Set the dish on a rack in the wok and add water to the level of the rack. Cover and steam until the scallops are white.

In the meantime, rinse and drain the bean sprouts. Shred the pepper or chilli and the shallot, and sauté together in about 1½ tablespoons of cooking oil with the remaining garlic until the bean sprouts have softened.

Add the premixed sauce ingredients and bring quickly to the boil. Drain the scallops and add to the bean sprouts. Heat through in the sauce, then serve.

# Fish with Black Beans and Vegetables

Make sure all scales are removed from fish

Add vegetables and flavourings, then steam

SERVES 4–6

2 × 400 g (13 oz) fresh whole fish (bream, snapper/ sea bass, porgy)
3 to 4 slices young fresh (root) ginger
⅓ stick celery
1 small carrot
30 g (1 oz) canned sliced bamboo shoots, drained
2 cloves garlic
1 tablespoon Chinese salted black beans
1 tablespoon dry sherry
2 teaspoons light soy sauce
2 teaspoons cooking oil

Clean and scale the fish. Make several cuts on each side of the fish to allow the seasonings to penetrate.

Peel and shred the ginger, celery and carrot. Shred the bamboo shoots. Finely chop the garlic and black beans.

Place the fish in a dish that will fit inside the wok. Scatter the prepared vegetables, black beans and garlic over the fish, then sprinkle on the remaining ingredients.

Set on a rack in the wok, add water to the level of the rack, and cover. Bring to the boil and steam gently for about 18 minutes. Serve.

# Sweet Carrot Custards

*Add milk and flavourings to carrots and cook gently*

*Use gloves when removing hot foods from wok*

SERVES 6

**750 g (1½ lb) carrots**
**1¾ cups (14 fl oz) milk**
**¼ teaspoon ground cardamom**
**1 teaspoon honey**
**1 tablespoon sugar**

**Custard**
**½ teaspoon ground cinnamon**
**1½ tablespoons sugar**
**¼ teaspoon saffron powder (optional)**
**2 eggs**

Peel and slice the carrots. Place in a saucepan or wok, with the milk, cardamom, honey and sugar. Bring to the boil, reduce heat and simmer gently until the carrot is completely tender and the milk reduced. Mash or purée in a blender or food processor, until smooth.

Beat the custard ingredients together, then stir into the carrot mixture. Grease six heatproof dessert dishes and pour the mixture into them.

Cover each with a piece of buttered aluminium foil.

Set on a rack in the wok, add water to the level of the rack and cover tightly. Steam over gently boiling water for 25 minutes until softly set. Serve hot or warm in the cups with whipped cream and toasted flaked almonds. Remember to use gloves when removing dishes from wok.

# Little Ginger Puddings

SERVES 6

**1½ cups (6 oz) self-raising flour**
**90 g (3 oz) butter**
**⅓ cup (3 oz) caster (powdered) sugar**
**¼ cup (1½ oz) chopped ginger preserved in syrup**
**2 eggs, beaten**
**¼ cup (2 fl oz) lukewarm milk**
**¼ cup (2 fl oz) syrup from preserved ginger**

Sift the flour onto a piece of paper. Cream the butter and sugar together, then add the ginger and beat well. Add the eggs, mixing thoroughly, then the sifted flour. Lastly stir in just enough of the milk to make a mixture of soft dropping consistency.

Pour a little of the ginger syrup into the bottom of each of six buttered single-serving pudding basins or other heatproof dishes. Divide the batter between the dishes and cover each with a piece of buttered aluminium foil.

Set on a rack in the wok and add water to just above the rack. Cover and steam for about 1 hour or until the puddings feel firm and springy to the touch and have loosened from the sides of the dishes. Turn out into dessert dishes and serve hot with whipped cream or custard.

Drained canned mandarin segments, heated in additional ginger syrup with a touch of slivered ginger, transforms this simple steamed pudding into a memorable dessert.

*Pour a little ginger syrup into each basin*

# Crème Caramel

SERVES 6

**2½ cups (20 fl oz) milk**
**½ cup (4 oz) sugar**
**3 eggs**
**1 egg yolk**
**pinch of salt**
**¾ teaspoon vanilla essence**

**Caramel**
**½ cup (4 oz) sugar**
**1 tablespoon water**

Heat the milk and sugar together, stirring until sugar dissolves and the milk is just warm. Remove from the heat. Beat the eggs and yolk lightly together and add the salt. Stir into the milk, and then beat with an electric or hand beater for about 3 minutes. Add the vanilla, then set aside.

Place the caramel ingredients in a saucepan. Set over moderate heat and stir occasionally until the sugar is dissolved, then allow the syrup to bubble gently until it turns a light golden colour. Pour into a dish that will hold about 3½ cups (28 fl oz) and swirl so that the toffee coats the bottom of the tin and runs half-way up the sides.

Pour in the custard, cover with a piece of aluminium foil pierced in several places, then set on a rack in the wok. Cover and steam over gently boiling water for about 25 minutes, or until the custard is set. Turn out on to a serving dish and chill thoroughly before serving with whipped cream.

If preferred, the custards can be cooked in smaller individual-serving tins (pans). These will require only about 18 minutes cooking time, but otherwise should be prepared in the same way as the larger custard.

*Swirl caramel in dish to coat evenly*

*Pierce foil to allow steam to escape*

# Lemon Egg Custard

SERVES 6

**6 whole eggs**
**3 egg whites**
**1½ cups (12 fl oz) milk**
**1½ tablespoons clear honey**
**2 teaspoons cornflour (cornstarch)**
**¾ teaspoon grated lemon rind (peel)**

**Topping**
**1 lemon**
**2 tablespoons sugar**
**½ cup (4 fl oz) water**

Beat the eggs and egg whites together. Add the milk, honey and cornflour and beat until smooth. Stir in the lemon rind.

Pour the mixture into six oiled heatproof dishes. Cover with aluminium foil and set on a rack in the steamer. Add water to just below the rack, cover and steam over gently boiling water for about 15 minutes until the custards are set.

In the meantime, peel the lemon and very finely shred the lemon rind after scraping away the pith. Place in a saucepan with the sugar and water and bring to a slow boil. Stir until the sugar has dissolved, then simmer gently until the syrup turns a light golden colour and is slightly sticky. Add about 1 tablespoon of lemon juice and stir on moderate heat until any toffee lumps that form have dissolved. Pour a little over each custard and serve hot.

If preferred, omit the lemon juice from the toffee. Chill the custards, top with the toffee and chill again until hard. Serve cold with whipped cream.

*Pour custard into heatproof bowls*

*Scrape white pith away from lemon rind, then shred*

*Add lemon juice to the sugar syrup*

# Babas au Kirsch

MAKES 10

2 cups (8 oz) flour
1 sachet dried yeast
   granules (7 g/1½
   teaspoons)
150 ml (5 fl oz) lukewarm
   milk
2 tablespoons caster
   (powdered) sugar
4 egg yolks
grated rind (peel) of
   ½ lemon
125 g (4 oz) butter
   (preferably clarified)
fresh strawberries
   (approx. 440 g (14 oz))
whipped cream
Kirsch

Syrup
2 cups (500 g/1 lb) sugar
2 cups (16 fl oz) water
2 tablespoons Kirsch

*Add spongy yeast mixture to flour*

*Slowly work butter into the dough*

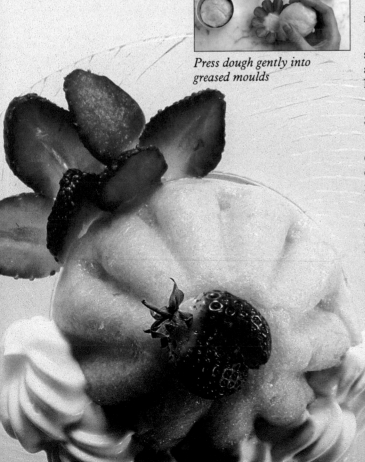

*Press dough gently into greased moulds*

Sift the flour into a mixing bowl and set in a warm place.

Sprinkle the yeast over ¼ cup (2 fl oz) of the milk, whisk with a fork, and leave for about 12 minutes until dissolved and beginning to bubble. Then add 1 teaspoon of the sugar and 1 tablespoon of the flour, mix in well, and leave until the mixture becomes spongy.

Beat the remaining sugar, the egg yolks and lemon rind together and set aside.

Melt the butter gently in a small saucepan, then remove from the heat and allow to settle. Pour off the butter fat, leaving the white residue behind. If using clarified butter, simply melt gently and set aside.

Make a well in the flour, and pour in the yeast and egg mixtures. Mix in lightly, then gradually add the remaining milk, working to a soft dough. Use your hands to knead the dough in the basin. Slowly add the butter, kneading and folding the dough until all the butter is incorporated and the dough is soft, shiny and smooth. When ready it should no longer stick to the fingers. Cover and leave in a warm place until doubled in volume.

Select 10 small baba moulds, brioche tins or heatproof dishes, and brush with melted butter. Divide the dough into 10 equal portions and press gently into the moulds. Set aside uncovered, until well risen.

Hull the strawberries, reserving 10 for decoration. Slice the remainder, then chill.

Pour the sugar and water for the syrup into a saucepan and stir slowly until the sugar has dissolved, then leave to boil for about 6 minutes until just slightly sticky. Remove from the heat and leave to cool, then add the Kirsch.

Prepare the whipped cream and flavour it with Kirsch. Set aside.

Place the *babas* on a rack in the wok, add water to the level of the rack and cover with the lid. Bring to the boil and steam over rapidly boiling water for 15 to 18 minutes until the cakes feel dry and springy.

Remove from the wok and turn them on to a cake rack to cool. Puncture all over with a sharp skewer. When cooled, place the *babas* in a dish and pour on the syrup. Refrigerate until quite cold.

To assemble, transfer the *babas* to individual dessert dishes. Top with the strawberries, placing a whole strawberry in the centre, then surround with the whipped cream.

# Traditional Plum Pudding

SERVES 8–12

250 g (8 oz) raisins
250 g (8 oz) sultanas
  (seedless raisins)
250 g (8 oz) currants
250 g (8 oz) grated suet
125 g (4 oz) fresh (soft)
  brown breadcrumbs
60 g (2 oz) candied peel
30 g (1 oz) slivered
  almonds
1 cooking apple, peeled
  and sliced
1 cup (8 oz) brown sugar
1 teaspoon salt
2 teaspoons ground mixed
  spice
1 teaspoon ground
  cinnamon
¼ teaspoon grated
  nutmeg
2 eggs, well beaten
1 lemon
1 orange
1½ tablespoons brandy
  or rum
1 cup (4 oz) flour

**Rum Butter**
125 g (4 oz) butter
  (preferably unsalted)
250 g (8 oz) soft dark
  brown sugar
2 tablespoons dark rum
¼ teaspoon grated
  nutmeg

*Add suet, crumbs and flavourings to fruit*

*Turn mixture into a greased pudding basin*

*Knot corners of prepared pudding cloth together*

Wash the dried fruits and dry thoroughly. Place in a mixing bowl and add the suet, crumbs, peel, almonds, apple and sugar, and mix thoroughly. Add the salt, spices and eggs, and mix well. Grate the rind (peel) of the lemon and orange, then squeeze the juice. Add to the mixture with the remaining ingredients and mix thoroughly.

Pour the mixture into a well-greased 1½ litre (6 cup) pudding basin. Cover with a piece of greased greaseproof paper, tied securely in place with string. Then cover with a scalded and floured pudding cloth and tie in place.

Set the basin on a rack in the wok, add water to half-way up the sides of the basin, and bring to the boil. Cover and steam over gently boiling water for 6 to 7 hours. Ensure that the water is topped up from time to time during cooking.

Lift out and leave to cool for a few minutes, then remove the pudding cloth. Uncover the pudding and turn out on to a serving plate. Cut into wedges, and serve hot with custard, brandy or rum butter or whipped cream. The pudding may be flamed with warmed liquor before serving.

To make the Rum Butter, beat the sugar and butter together until soft and light, then add the rum and nutmeg. Chill until firm before serving. Rum Butter can be kept for several weeks in the refrigerator.

Cooked plum puddings can be kept for several months before use. Wrap in several layers of aluminium foil and store in a cool cupboard. Steam for about 1½ hours before serving, the longer you steam it, the darker it becomes.

# Orange Pudding

SERVES 6–8

**1½ cups (6 oz) self-raising (self-rising) flour**
**90 g (3 oz) butter**
**⅓ cup (3 oz) caster (powdered) sugar**
**2 eggs, beaten**
**2 tablespoons orange jam/marmalade**
**1 teaspoon grated orange rind (peel)**
**approx ¼ cup (2 fl oz) warm milk**

**Orange Custard**
**2 cups (16 fl oz) freshly squeezed orange juice**
**½ teaspoon grated orange rind (peel)**
**4 egg yolks**
**¼ cup (2 oz) caster (powdered) sugar**
**2 teaspoons cornflour (cornstarch)**
**1 tablespoon cold water**

Sift the flour into a mixing bowl. Cream the butter and sugar together until light and creamy. Add the beaten eggs and the jam or marmalade and mix well. Add the rind. Fold in the sifted flour and mix thoroughly. Add just enough warm milk to make a soft dropping consistency.

Grease a pudding basin or eight custard cups and pour in the mixture. Cover with a piece of greased greaseproof paper and set on a rack in the wok.

Add water to just above the rack, cover and steam over gently boiling water for about 1¼ hours for a large pudding or 30 minutes for small puddings.

When the pudding is done, it will begin to come away from the sides of the basin. Let it stand for about 5 minutes, then turn out on to a serving plate. Serve hot with Orange Custard, or with cream and marmalade topping—marmalade heated with butter until it just reaches boiling point.

To make the Orange Custard, place the orange juice in a saucepan and heat until almost boiling. Then remove from the heat and leave to cool.

Beat the orange rind, egg yolks and sugar together until creamy. Mix the cornflour and cold water together, then beat into the egg mixture. Stand the dish on a rack in the wok with water around the bottom of the dish barely simmering. Gradually add the orange juice to tne eggs, beating briskly until the custard is thick enough to coat the back of a spoon. Serve hot with the Orange Pudding.

*Add warm milk to batter to make a soft consistency*

*Turn into basins and steam, covered with foil*

# Braising

The Chinese never considered the wok as the important pan for braising and stewing. This was usually done in a deep pottery pot over a small clay charcoal-burning stove.

But its possibilities as a stewpan should not be overlooked. To begin with, it is larger than most pans in the domestic kitchen, making it invaluable for those times when you're faced with the task of cooking for a crowd. It can be used to cook a large whole joint—say, a leg of lamb or pork, or even a whole turkey—utilizing its domed lid to create extra capacity. It handles the preliminary browning/searing that should be done before meat begins to stew, with ease and efficiency.

Its success as a braising/stewing pan, however, depends primarily on the flexibility of the heat source beneath it. In this instance, gas, which is so eminently suitable for quick stir-frying, often cannot be regulated to offer the low-simmering temperatures required for braising. If your gas cooker does not have a very low-regulating ring, the problem can be overcome by placing the wok on a *wok stand* to raise it slightly above the gas ring. This introduces a cooling air buffer between the wok and its heat source. Some electric cookers, particularly those fitted with hotplates, may also require a wok stand to modify the cooking temperature.

Wok stands are readily available where woks and other Chinese cooking equipment are sold. They are particularly necessary if you intend to use your wok as a deep-fryer as well, because it is essential to have a steady base on which to rest a hot wok, filled with cooking oil, after use.

Stainless steel and aluminium woks are perhaps more suited to braising than iron or steel woks. I have noticed on occasion that my braised dishes have acquired a hint of a metallic taste when cooked in my standard wok, particularly dishes with acidic sauces such as those cooked with wine or citrus juices. I have found, in fact, that an electric wok is very well suited to braising. The Teflon coating on the interior prevents sticking as well as eliminating the possibility of contamination of flavours.

Braising is simple. The meat should be browned and sealed before stewing to prevent it drying out, shrinking and thus becoming tough, and also to lend colour to both the meat and the resultant sauce.

Have the wok on fairly high heat, add cooking oil, fat or butter, and then brown the meat, several pieces at a time, turning to ensure that all surfaces are evenly coloured. Do not overcrowd the wok at this stage or the meat will not colour sufficiently. Remove each piece when done, and brown the remainder in batches, then return the meat to the pan and add the remaining ingredients. Bring the liquid just to the boil, then reduce the heat and simmer for the required cooking time. The fragments of meat that adhere to the pan during browning will flake off during cooking to add flavour and colour to the sauce.

When braising poultry, the wings and breasts may be added to the pan after the remainder has been partially cooked, to prevent them overcooking.

Liquids added to meat for stewing/braising should be lukewarm or even hot—never ice cold as this can cause the meat to toughen. If additional liquid is to be added to the dish during cooking, this must always be warm or hot.

# Celery in Mustard Sauce

SERVES 4–6

**4 sticks fresh celery (approx. 220 g/7 oz)**
**2 tablespoons butter**
**¾ cup (6 fl oz) chicken stock**
**¼ cup (2 fl oz) milk**
**1½ teaspoons prepared hot mustard**
**2 teaspoons flour**
**1 egg yolk**
**2 tablespoons thickened (heavy) cream**
**salt and black pepper**

Wash the celery and cut into 10 cm (4 in) pieces. Sauté in
1½ tablespoons of the butter until beginning to soften
(about 3 minutes). Add the chicken stock, milk and mustard.
Cover and simmer gently for about 20 minutes.

Remove the celery to a serving plate. Mix the flour and
remaining butter together and stir into the sauce to thicken.
Beat the egg yolk and cream together lightly and add to the
sauce off the heat. Beat briskly until smooth and thick.
Season to taste and pour over the celery. Serve at once.

Wash celery and cut into
lengths

Add butter and
flour to sauce

# Braised Red Cabbage

SERVES 4

**410 g (13 oz) red cabbage**
**1 tablespoon butter**
**1 medium onion, finely chopped**
**¼ cup (2 oz) sugar**
**1 cooking apple, sliced**
**1 tablespoon white vinegar**
**¼ cup (2 fl oz) water**
**1 teaspoon salt**
**⅓ teaspoon caraway seeds**

Shred the cabbage, discarding the outer leaves and core.
Heat the butter in the wok and sauté the onion until
transparent. Add the sugar, apple, vinegar and water and
bring to the boil. Add the cabbage, cover the wok and braise
gently for about 1 hour.

Season with the salt and caraway seeds about 15 minutes
before the cabbage is ready.

Discard core and outer
leaves and shred cabbage

Add cabbage to wok and
braise until cooked

# Leeks in Tomato and Parsley Sauce

**SERVES 4–6**

**6 fresh leeks
1 medium onion, sliced
2 tablespoons olive oil
1 large tomato,
   chopped
1 tablespoon tomato paste,
   purée or powder
¼ cup chopped parsley
¾ cup (6 fl oz) water
salt and black pepper
lemon juice**

Remove the coarse outer leaves from the leeks and trim off the root, cutting from two sides to form a point. Split the white parts down the centre. This preparation makes it easier to clean the leeks. Wash thoroughly in cold water and drain.

Sauté the onion in the oil until transparent. Then add the tomato and sauté until softened. Stir in the tomato paste and half the parsley and add the water. Bring to the boil, cover the wok and simmer for 7 to 8 minutes.

Add the leeks, cover again and braise gently until the leeks are tender (about 20 minutes). Add salt, pepper and lemon juice to taste and then stir in the remaining parsley. Serve hot or well chilled.

*Split leeks down centre for washing*

*Wash under running cold water to remove all grit*

*Add leeks to tomato mixture, then braise*

# Boeuf Bourguignon

SERVES 4–6

**750 g (1½ lb) good stewing steak**
**½ bottle (1½ cups/12 fl oz) good red wine**
**1 bouquet garni (bunch of fresh herbs)**
**4 black peppercorns**
**125 g (4 oz) pickled (salt) pork or bacon**
**12 small (pickling) onions**
**1½ tablespoons lard (pork fat)**
**1 tablespoon flour**
**⅓ teaspoon grated nutmeg**
**salt and black pepper**

Trim the steak and cut into small cubes. Place in a dish with the wine, herbs and peppercorns, cover with plastic wrap and leave for about 5 hours.

Cut the pork or bacon into small cubes. Peel the onions. Heat the lard in the wok and fry the pork and onions until the pork is quite crisp and the onions coloured. Remove and set aside.

Drain the meat, reserving the marinade, and fry in the remaining fat until evenly coloured. Cook in two or three batches to avoid stewing.

Sprinkle on the flour and leave to colour slightly, then return all the meat, the pork and onions, and add the nutmeg and a dash of salt and pepper. Pour in the reserved marinade and bring to the boil. Cover tightly and simmer gently for about 2 hours on moderate to low heat. Shake the wok from time to time to turn the meat. If preferred, the onions can be added in the last 30 minutes of cooking to prevent them overcooking.

*Marinate meat in wine and herbs for 5 hours*

*Fry salt pork and peeled onions until crisp*

*Braise gently, stirring occasionally*

# Greek-style Beef

## Sofrito

SERVES 6

**1¼ kg (2½ lb) blade or round beef steak**
**¾ cup (3 oz) flour**
**1½ teaspoons salt**
**½ teaspoon ground black pepper**
**¼ cup (2 fl oz) olive oil**
**1 tablespoon butter**
**2–4 cloves garlic, crushed**
**¼ cup (2 fl oz) wine vinegar**
**¼ cup (2 fl oz) red wine**
**1 teaspoon sugar**
**1½ tablespoons chopped parsley**
**1 cup (8 fl oz) water or beef stock**

Cut the meat into cubes. Mix the flour, salt and pepper together in a plastic or paper bag, and add the meat. Shake briskly until the meat is evenly coated, then transfer to a colander and shake off any excess flour.

Heat the olive oil and butter in the wok, and brown the meat in several batches until evenly coloured. Add the garlic, and cook briefly. Return all the meat, add the vinegar and wine, bring almost to the boil, then simmer for 3 minutes. Add the sugar, parsley and water, cover the wok and simmer gently for about 1¼ hours until the meat is completely tender and will cut with a fork.

Serve with mashed potatoes or boiled pasta and sautéed spinach or other green vegetables.

*Shake cubed meat in a bag to coat with flour*

*Brown meat in several batches*

# Goulash

SERVES 4

**625 g (1¼ lb) veal steak**
**2 tablespoons olive oil or cooking oil**
**1 medium onion, finely chopped**
**¾ teaspoon sweet paprika**
**salt**
**½ cup (4 fl oz) water**
**½ cup (4 fl oz) sour cream**

Cut the veal into small cubes and sauté in two or three batches in the oil until evenly coloured. Remove and keep warm.

Add the onion and fry until lightly coloured and softened. Return the meat and add the paprika and salt. Pour in about ½ cup of water, cover the wok and braise gently for about 1½ hours until the meat is completely tender.

Add a splash of hot water from time to time during cooking to prevent the dish drying up and sticking to the pan. Just before serving stir in the sour cream and heat through.

*Add paprika and salt to browned veal and onion in wok*

*Add sour cream to goulash just before serving and heat through*

# Lamb Korma

SERVES 4

1 kg (2 lb) shoulder or leg lamb
2 medium onions
2 tablespoons ghee (clarified butter)
1 tablespoon ground coriander
1½ teaspoons ground cummin
½ teaspoon chilli powder
2–3 cloves garlic, chopped
1½ teaspoons grated fresh (root) ginger
2 tablespoons ground almonds
200 ml (¾ cup) natural yoghurt
1 teaspoon salt
¼ teaspoon ground black pepper

Cut the lamb into cubes discarding bones and fat.
Thinly slice 1 onion and grate or chop the other.

Fry the lamb in the ghee until evenly coloured. Add the
onions and fry until these are coloured. Then add the spices,
garlic and ginger, and fry briefly. Add the ground almonds
and the yoghurt and braise gently until the liquid has been
absorbed (about 25 minutes).

Add salt and pepper and enough water to just cover the
meat. Cover and braise gently until the meat is very tender
(about 45 minutes). Shake the wok occasionally to turn the
meat, but keep the lid on
throughout the cooking.
Serve with saffron rice
and a spicy chutney.

*Cut lamb into cubes,
discarding bones and fat*

*Fry lamb in ghee (clarified
butter) in wok*

*Add yoghurt to curry
mixture and braise gently*

# Lamb Rolls Stuffed with Apple and Coriander

SERVES 4

This innovative use of lamb loin cutlets can be served as a main course, or sliced and served hot or cold as an appetizer.

2 loins (racks) of lamb, each of 6 cutlets
   (approx. 500 g/1 lb)
¾ cooking apple
½ tablespoon ground coriander
½ cup (2 oz) seasoned flour
1 tablespoon cooking oil
2 tablespoons butter
1¼ cups (10 fl oz) apple juice or cider
2 teaspoons chopped parsley

Bone out the loins and trim away excess fat. Peel and slice the apple. Season the inside of the loins with the coriander and plenty of salt and pepper. Place the sliced apple along the centre of each. Roll up the lamb with the meaty 'eye' section inside. Tie securely with clean string. Roll in the seasoned flour, coating lightly.

Heat the oil and butter together in the wok and sauté the lamb rolls until well and evenly coloured. Pour off the fat and add the apple juice. Bring just to the boil then reduce the heat, cover and braise for about 30 minutes until the lamb is just cooked through and the juice reduced to a tangy dark glaze on the meat. Shake the pan from time to time during cooking to turn the rolls to ensure that they are evenly cooked and glazed.

Transfer to a serving plate after cutting each roll in half through the centre. Pour on any remaining glaze and garnish with the chopped parsley.

*Trim all fat away from boned loins of lamb*

*Place apple slices in the seasoned lamb*

*Roll up and tie with string*

*Add apple juice to the browned meat and braise*

# Lebanese Orange Duck

SERVES 6–8

**1 × 2.2 kg (4½ lb) duck**
**1 large onion, chopped**
**2½ tablespoons butter**
**3 large oranges**
**½ lemon**
**salt and black pepper**
**1 tablespoon flour**
**1 tablespoon toasted**
**    almonds**

*Brown duck on all sides, turning with two wooden spoons to protect skin*

*Pour in orange and lemon juice and braise the duck until tender*

*Duck may be served whole or cut into serving pieces*

Clean and dress the duck. Sauté the onion in the butter until lightly coloured. Push to one side of the pan and put in the duck. Brown gently all over, turning it with two wooden spoons to avoid breaking the skin. Pour off the fat.

Squeeze 2 oranges and the lemon for juice and pour the juice over the duck. Add salt and pepper, cover the wok and braise gently for about 1½ hours until completely tender. The pan juices should be reduced to a rich dark glaze. Turn the duck several times to ensure even cooking.

When done, remove the duck from the wok.

Sprinkle the flour into the wok and add the juice of the remaining orange. Bring to the boil, stirring, then cook until the sauce is thick. If the duck is a fat one, pour off most of the fat that will have accumulated in the wok before making the sauce. Serve the duck on a platter garnished with orange slices and parsley and carve at the table. Alternatively cut the duck into 6 to 8 pieces and arrange on a serving dish garnished with toasted almonds.

# Coq au Vin

SERVES 6

**1 × 1.5 kg (3 lb) roasting chicken**
**2 rashers bacon**
**12 small (pickling) onions**
**24 small fresh mushrooms**
**1½ tablespoons butter**
**1½ tablespoons olive oil or cooking oil**
**salt and black pepper**
**½ cup (2 oz) flour**
**2 cloves garlic, chopped**
**2 tablespoons brandy**
**2 cups (16 fl oz) good red wine**
**1 cup (8 fl oz) chicken stock**
**2 sprigs parsley**
**⅓ teaspoon dried thyme**
**2 bay leaves**
**1 tablespoon flour**
**½ teaspoon sugar**
**2 tablespoons chopped parsley**

Wash the chicken and wipe dry. Cut into six pieces: two leg and thigh portions, two wing and breast portions and two lower breast sections. Dice the bacon. Peel the onions. Trim the mushrooms.

Heat the butter and oil together in the wok. Add the bacon, sauté until beginning to crisp, then remove. Add the onions and cook until lightly coloured; add the mushrooms and cook until beginning to soften. Remove.

Season the chicken pieces with salt and pepper, then coat lightly with flour. Cook two pieces at a time, until evenly coloured.

When all are done, return the chicken, bacon and vegetables to the wok and add the garlic. Cover and braise gently for about 15 minutes.

Remove the chicken and other ingredients from the wok and skim off the fat. Warm the brandy in a ladle and flame, pour into the wok and extinguish with the wine and stock. Bring to the boil, add the herbs, flour, sugar and a little extra butter, and whisk vigorously until smooth. Boil until the sauce is reduced by one-third.

Return the chicken and other ingredients. Cover the wok and braise for about 45 minutes until the chicken is tender. The sauce should be sufficiently thick by this time.

Stir in the chopped parsley, check the seasonings, and serve.

*Cut chicken into six pieces, then coat with flour*

*Add mushrooms to browned onions in wok*

*Remove chicken from wok*

# Outdoor Cooking

I remember a time when my good saucepans, kettle and frying pan would be returned from a camping spree blackened with smoke, and with handles badly charred. No longer, however, since I acquired an inexpensive rolled-steel wok to take instead. It functions as frying pan, stew pot, oven and kettle all in one. And the only other pieces of equipment I find necessary to pack are its lid, a metal rack to use should we decide to do a little steaming or smoking, a good-sized ladle and the 'charn' spatula.

My camp-fire wok begins its day as a kettle to boil water for a mug of coffee or pot of tea, and there's plenty of hot water left over for my husband's shave or to do the previous night's dishes. A rinse and rub-out with a piece of crumpled kitchen paper, and it's ready for omelettes, or eggs and bacon, or porridge, or to receive those promised freshly caught fish.

Then throughout the day, it remains busy—frying up noodles, stewing meat and vegetables, poaching, steaming, boiling—with no more care needed than a brisk scrub at the nearest source of clean water. And last thing at night after the meal is finished and the campsite put in order, we might relax around the fading fire to mull a bottle of red wine, adding cloves, orange zest, cinnamon and a good big dash of brandy.

When the wok is used at the campsite, it sits directly into a bed of glowing coals, or is supported over the fire on a ring of rocks or wood blocks. Its looped metal handles cannot be damaged through too-close acquaintance with the fire; and its bottom, though soon pitch-black, will be unmarked.

We're a little more sophisticated when we cook out of doors at home. An old tray-mobile, found at a second-hand store and refurbished, now holds my gas wok-cooker on top, gas bottle below, and has a drawer for the various wok paraphernalia, as well as plenty of space beside the cooker for preparation. This can be wheeled to any corner of the garden that looks particularly inviting, and there we relax with a bottle of wine while *paella*, vegetable soup or meaty stew bubbles happily in the wok at our side.

The wok for outdoor cooking is practical and, to me, now indispensable.

# Spanish Omelette

SERVES 4

2 large potatoes
2 medium onions
1 red or green capsicum (bell pepper)
2 tablespoons olive oil
1 tablespoon butter
2 teaspoons finely chopped parsley*
½ teaspoon chopped fresh oregano or sage*
¾ teaspoon salt
pinch of ground black pepper
3 eggs, beaten

Tomato Sauce
1 medium onion, finely chopped
1 clove garlic, chopped
2 tablespoons finely chopped celery
1½ tablespoons butter
2 tablespoons finely chopped mushrooms
2 medium tomatoes, peeled and chopped
¾ teaspoon salt
large pinch of ground black pepper
1 teaspoon sugar
⅔ cup (5 fl oz) chicken stock or water

Peel the potatoes and onions and cut into small dice. Remove stem, seed pod and inner ribs from the capsicum and cut into small squares or narrow strips.

Heat the oil and butter in the wok and put in the vegetables. Sauté gently, covered, for about 15 minutes until the potatoes are just tender. Shake the pan from time to time to turn the vegetables, and stir if needed to prevent sticking.

Add the herbs, salt and pepper, and mix in lightly. Pour on the beaten eggs and leave to cook very gently until firm. Serve immediately with fresh tomato sauce.

To make the Tomato Sauce, place the onion, garlic and celery in a saucepan or wok with the butter; cover and cook gently for about 7 minutes. Add the mushrooms and cook for a further 2 to 3 minutes. Add the chopped tomato, stir; then season with the salt, pepper and sugar, and cook for 3 to 4 minutes. Add the stock or water and simmer gently for about 15 minutes until the sauce is thick. It may be passed through a sieve to produce a smooth sauce, if preferred.

*  *If fresh herbs are unavailable, use half quantities of dried herbs.*

*Sauté vegetables until tender*

*Add herbs and seasonings to vegetables*

*Pour in beaten eggs and cook gently*

# Paella

SERVES 6

3 cups (500 g / 1 lb) raw long-grain rice
½ cup (4 fl oz) olive oil
⅓ teaspoon saffron powder
1½ teaspoons salt
3 Chorizo sausages
2 large rashers (slices) streaky (fat) bacon, or 2 slices
    raw smoked ham
1 medium onion, chopped
185 g (6 oz) boneless chicken
185 g (6 oz) fish fillets
6 large green prawns (raw shrimps) in the shell
12 stoned black olives
5½–6 cups (1.5 litres) water or chicken stock
1 green capsicum (bell pepper)
1 red capsicum (bell pepper)
½ cup frozen green peas, thawed
12 clams or mussels, in the shell
1 medium-sized sand crab (approx. 315 g / 10 oz)

Place the rice in the wok with the olive oil, saffron and salt, and sauté until the rice turns a light golden colour. Add the sliced *Chorizo* sausage, diced bacon or ham and the onion, and continue to sauté, stirring continually, until the bacon begins to crisp and the onion is lightly coloured.

Cut the chicken and fish into cubes. Add to the wok with the prawns, washed but not shelled, and the olives. Add about 5½ cups water or chicken stock and bring briskly to the boil, stirring; reduce the heat, cover the wok and simmer very gently.

Remove stems, seed pods and inner ribs from the peppers and cut them into small squares. Add to the rice, together with the peas, scrubbed clams or mussels and the crab which has been cut into large pieces and inedible parts removed. Re-cover the wok and leave to simmer for a further 8 to 10 minutes until the rice and all ingredients are tender.

Stir so that the meat and vegetables are evenly distributed in the rice. Serve in large bowls.

*Add sausage, bacon and onion to rice in wok*

*Add chicken, fish, prawns and olives*

*Pour in water or chicken stock and simmer.*

*Add mussels and crab to other ingredients in wok*

# Prawns Cooked in Salt

SERVES 6 AS AN APPETIZER OR MAIN COURSE

**6 very large green king prawns (large raw shrimp),
    in their shells (each approx. 220 g/7 oz)
1 kg (2 lb) rock (sea) salt**

**Sauce
¼ cup (2 fl oz) light soy sauce
1 fresh red chilli, chopped
1 tablespoon cooking oil**

Cut down prawn through
centre back shell and remove
vein

Heat salt in foil-lined wok,
add prawns and cover with
remaining salt

Trim the prawn legs. Cut down the centre backs through the
shells and pull away the intestinal veins.

Line the wok with a piece of aluminium foil and put in the
salt. Cover the wok and heat until the salt is quite hot to the
touch. Remove half the salt, smooth flat and place the prawns
on the remaining salt. Cover with the salt that was removed.
Cover the wok and cook over moderate heat for about
12 minutes. The cooked meat should be firm and
white. Do not overcook.

Mix the sauce ingredients together and pour
into small dishes. Brush the salt off the prawns.
Serve with lemon wedges and the sauce.

# Catch of the Day

SERVES 2

**2 freshly caught fish
    (whiting, perch, snapper)
2 tablespoons flour
salt and black pepper
juice of ½ lemon
60 g (2 oz) butter
parsley**

Clean and scale the fish and wash well; dry with a kitchen
towel. Mix the flour, salt and pepper together. Score each
side of the fish lightly in several places and sprinkle on a
little lemon juice. Coat lightly with the seasoned flour.

Melt the butter in the wok until it begins to foam. Put in
the fish and fry on moderate heat on each side for about
3 minutes, turning carefully. Sprinkle with the remaining
lemon juice, garnish with parsley, and serve at once.

Score fish and sprinkle with
lemon juice

Coat lightly with seasoned
flour

# Quick Sourdough Bread

SERVES 6

**3 cups (12 oz) white or wholemeal (wholewheat)
self-raising (self-rising) flour
2 cups (16 fl oz) buttermilk, or a mixture of water
and plain yoghurt
1 teaspoon salt
½ cup (3 oz) sultanas (seedless raisins), optional**

Sift the flour into a mixing bowl and add the buttermilk
(or yoghurt and water) and the salt. Mix thoroughly,
then add the sultanas, if used, and mix in.

Thickly butter a large sheet of aluminium foil, then cut
another piece of foil of the same size. Place the dough in the
centre of the buttered foil and seal, allowing room for
expansion. Wrap this in the unbuttered foil.

Place a metal rack in the wok and set the wok over gently
glowing coals. Place the parcel on the rack, cover the wok and
cook gently for about 30 minutes, then turn and cook for a
further 30 minutes or until the bread is cooked through,
dry and springy to the touch. Serve with lashings of butter.

*Turn dough onto a sheet of
thickly buttered foil*

*Seal edges allowing room for
expansion*

# German Apple Pancake
## *Apfelpfannkuchen*

SERVES 4–6

Despite its lengthy name, this pan-cooked apple cake/ pancake is quick and easy to do.

**2 large green (cooking) apples**
**¼ cup (1½ oz) sultanas (seedless raisins)**
**1 tablespoon caster (powdered) sugar**
**1 teaspoon ground cinnamon**
**90 g (3 oz) butter**
**1 tablespoon brandy (optional)**
**3 eggs**
**¼ cup (1 oz) flour**
**⅓ cup (2½ fl oz) milk**
**1 tablespoon sugar**
**pinch of salt**
**2 teaspoons soft brown sugar (optional)**

Peel, core and slice the apples. Place in the wok with the sultanas, sugar, cinnamon and half the butter. Cover and cook very gently for about 7 minutes until the apple is tender. Increase the heat, splash in the brandy if used, and cook for a further 1 minute. Transfer to a plate and rinse out the wok.

Beat the eggs with the flour and milk for 2 minutes, then add the sugar and salt and beat again until dissolved.

Melt the remaining butter in the wok and pour in the batter. Cover and cook very gently for 10 minutes.

Spread the apples over the top of the pancake, re-cover the wok and cook for a further 12 to 15 minutes until the pancake is firm and slightly puffed. Do not allow it to cook too quickly. Slide the pancake on to a plate and sprinkle on the brown sugar, if used. Serve at once. If liked decorate with whipped cream and cinnamon.

*Cook apples in covered wok until tender*

*Spread apples over cooked batter*

# Pancakes with Maple Syrup

SERVES 4

Pancakes never taste better than when eaten out of doors. An iron wok nestled into coals should cook them perfectly.

**2¼ cups (9 oz) wholemeal or white self-raising (self-rising) flour**
**60 g (2 oz) sugar**
**small pinch of salt**
**3 medium eggs, beaten**
**1⅓ cups (11 fl oz) milk**
**1 cup (8 fl oz) maple syrup or clear honey**
**butter, preferably unsalted**

Sift the flour into a mixing bowl and add the sugar and salt. Stir in the eggs and milk and beat for 2 minutes, then set aside for about 10 minutes to allow the flour to soften and the rising agents to activate.

Warm the syrup or honey in a small saucepan on the edge of the fire. Beat the butter with a fork until light and fluffy. Set aside.

Vigorously rub the interior of the wok with a piece of oiled kitchen paper until it appears smooth and has a dull shine.

Place the wok on the coals, and heat to moderate. Pour in a large spoonful of the batter and cook until the entire surface is covered with bubbles, then turn the pancake and cook the other side until it is golden.

Serve at once, or keep warm while the remaining pancakes are cooked. Spread with the butter and pour on the syrup before serving.

*Stir eggs and milk into flour to make a batter*

*Cook each pancake until golden on both sides*

# Mulled Red Wine

SERVES 4–6

**1 bottle red wine**
**1 stick cinnamon**
**3 cloves**
**1½ tablespoons sugar**
**1 cup (8 fl oz) brandy**
**orange rind (peel)**

Pour the wine into the wok and add the cinnamon and cloves. Heat gently. Mix the sugar and brandy together, stirring until the sugar dissolves. Pour into a metal ladle. Hold the orange rind above the wok with long-handled tongs. Flame the brandy, then slowly pour it down the orange rind so that it flows into the wine. Allow to heat briefly, then ladle into mugs or stem glasses wrapped in napkins.

*Add cinnamon and cloves to wine*

*Hold orange rind above wok and pour over brandy*

# Smoked Dishes

In the context of this collection of recipes, smoked foods are those that are smoke-cooked, not smoke-cured. The latter are foods, most commonly beef and fish, that have been subjected to a cool smoky enclosed atmosphere for a period of time (days or even weeks) to both dry-preserve and flavour them.

Smoke-cooking uses the heat generated from the cooking source to cook the food by indirect means, while simultaneously suffusing it with a strongly aromatic smoke. This smoky flavour thoroughly permeates the food, lending to it a fragrance and taste characteristic of the smoking ingredients used, these being predominantly naturally aromatic woods in the form of chips or shavings.

Hickory wood chips are a popular smoking fuel which is now available in many stores where barbecue equipment and fuel are sold. Additionally, we can utilize the smoke-fuel favoured by Chinese cooks for centuries: green or black tea leaves, dried orange or mandarin (tangerine) peel and sugar. They also use the highly aromatic camphor wood for smoking meats, particularly duck.

Not every type of fragrant wood can be used successfully for smoking. Pine and other resinous softwoods should not be used as they will create an unpleasant flavour that would ruin the food. But oak, poplar, fruit woods such as apple and orange, certain types of wattle (mimosa) and of course hickory and camphor can be used.

Fresh herbs also make aromatic smoke-fuel. Branches or large sprigs of fresh rosemary, bay laurel or thyme will give the meat an elusive flavour.

Smoke-cooking in a wok is simple. A heavy iron wok makes the ideal domestic smoke-cooker. It should remain unaffected through exposure to direct heat, where a cooking pot of less sturdy construction might buckle or burn. If an aluminium, stainless steel, Teflon-coated or electric wok is to be used, test it cautiously on moderate temperatures, to avoid damage.

The wok should preferably be used out of doors, either on a portable gas or electric ring, or over a charcoal or wood fire, as the smoke can be quite pervasive and acrid.

A double thickness of aluminium foil in the bottom of the wok will prevent burnt chips sticking to the pan and possibly spoiling the surface. The chips are placed directly on the foil, and a metal rack of open construction is placed over the chips, allowing space for the smoke to circulate. The food to be smoked is placed directly on the rack, which should be rubbed with oil to prevent sticking. Cuts of meat should be first sealed by quickly searing (browning) in the wok with a little cooking oil or beef dripping. This prevents the natural moisture of the meat being drawn out during the cooking/smoking process.

Meats, fish and poultry can be completely dry smoke-cooked. That is, they simply sit on the rack and cook slowly in the dry smoky heat generated below. Or they can be cooked in a combination of steam and smoke, by adding water to the smoke-fuel below the rack. The water will first create steam and then, as it evaporates, the smoke-fuel will dry out and eventually begin to smoke, to complete the cooking cycle with dry smoke heat. This method is particularly effective for delicate and lean meats such as chicken or quail which may become dried out by smoke-cooking alone.

# Chinese Smoked Chicken

SERVES 4

**1 × 1.2 kg (2½ lb) chicken**
**2 tablespoons Chinese black tea leaves**
**½ dried orange or mandarin (tangerine) rind (peel)**
**1 tablespoon sugar**

Wash the chicken and wipe dry. Set on a rack in the wok and add water to below the level of the rack. Cover and steam for about 45 minutes, turning twice.

Remove the chicken and the rack, and drain off the remaining water. Line the wok with a double thickness of aluminium foil and add the remaining ingredients.

Set over high heat until they begin to smoke. Then return the chicken on the rack, cover the wok and smoke over moderate heat until the chicken is cooked through and is a rich golden colour. Turn several times to colour evenly. Smoking time should be about 25 minutes.

Serve hot, or leave to cool and then slice thinly. Serve with mayonnaise and salad as a light luncheon dish.

*Steam chicken on a rack or in bamboo basket*

*Add tea, mandarin rind, sugar to foil-lined wok*

*When smoking place chicken on top of rack*

*Turn chicken several times to colour evenly*

# Duck Smoked with Camphor Wood and Tea Leaves

SERVES 4

The elaborate carving of linen chests made from camphor wood has been a respected art in China for many centuries. And this craft has always yielded a ready source of chips and shavings of fragrant wood. Placed in the bottom of the wok, they impart a rich golden-red colouring and delicate smoky flavour which combines particularly well with the rich taste of duck.

**1 × 1.5 kg (3 lb) duck**
**2 tablespoons Chinese black tea leaves**
**1 cup camphor wood chips★**
**2 cups (16 fl oz) water**

Wash the duck and wipe dry. Line the wok with a double thickness of aluminium foil and put in the tea leaves, wood chips and the water. Bring to the boil. Set a metal rack in the wok and place the duck on top. Cover and steam until the water has evaporated, then continue to cook for about 1¼ hours, turning the duck from time to time. After the water evaporates, the wood chips and tea leaves will dry out and begin to smoke, so the duck is cooked in a combination of steam and smoke—making it moist and aromatic and drawing out much of the excess fat.

★ *If unobtainable, hickory wood chips can be used.*

*Add water to tea leaves and wood in lined wok*

*Set duck on a metal rack over wood chip mixture*

*Chinese metal racks can be easily bent to desired height for greater convenience*

# Rosemary-smoked Steaks

SERVES 4

**4 sirloin (striploin/porterhouse) steaks,
each approx. 220 g (7 oz)
2 tablespoons beef dripping (fat) or cooking oil
and butter mixed
2–3 large sprigs fresh rosemary**

Trim the steaks if necessary. Heat the fat in the wok and
quickly brown the steaks on both sides to seal and colour.
Remove, then drain the wok and rinse.

Place the rosemary in the wok and set a rack over it.
Arrange the steaks on the rack. Cover the wok and smoke for
12 to 15 minutes until the steaks are cooked to individual
taste. Serve at once, garnished with rosemary.

The wok can also be used in conjunction with a barbecue
fire to make delectable grilled steaks with a smoky flavour.
Prepare a charcoal or wood-chip fire and allow it to burn
down to glowing coals. Set a rack over the fire and place the
steaks on top to sear quickly on both sides. Dampen branches
of fresh rosemary (or use handfuls of well-soaked hickory
chips) and place on the fire. Cover with an upturned wok
and allow the steaks to smoke until cooked to taste.

*Sear steaks, two at a time on
both sides*

*Place sprigs of rosemary in
foil-lined wok*

*Arrange steaks on a rack,
cover and smoke*

# Smoked Rumpsteak

SERVES 6–8

A tasty and unusual main course, smoked beef is also delicious served with aperitifs.

**1½ kg (3 lb) rump steak
1 cup hickory chips**

Trim excess fat from the steak. Rub the wok with an oiled cloth, then heat about 1 tablespoon of beef dripping (fat) or cooking oil. Sear the meat on all surfaces, then remove from the wok and rinse away the fat.

Line the interior of the wok with a double thickness of aluminium foil and put in the chips. Place the meat on a rack over the chips. Cover and set over high heat until the chips begin to smoke, then reduce the heat very slightly and continue to smoke for about 35 minutes or until the meat is cooked to taste. A meat thermometer can be used to test if the meat is done. Remove from the wok and allow to cool slightly. Slice thinly and serve hot topped with fried onion rings and herbs or cold, with mayonnaise, horseradish or mustard.

*Sear the rump steak on both sides*

*Place the meat on a rack over wood chips in foil-lined wok and cook over high heat*

# Smoked Fish

SERVES 4

This can be crisply deep-fried or eaten as it is.

**4 fillets sea perch or bream (see bass/porgy),
   approx. 100 g/3½ oz each
2 tablespoons green tea leaves
1½ tablespoons light soy sauce
2 teaspoons dry sherry or ginger wine
½ teaspoon Chinese spiced salt**

Place the fish fillets on a smoking rack. Line the
wok with a double thickness of aluminium foil
and put in the tea leaves. Set the rack in place.
Brush the fish with the soy sauce and sherry or
wine on both sides. Cover the wok and smoke
the fish for 10 minutes.

   Serve straight from the pan with a soy sauce
and spiced salt dip.

*Brush fish fillets with soy
sauce and wine*

*Fish will take about
10 minutes to smoke*

# Thai Smoked Crabs

SERVES 4

I enjoyed my first taste of smoked crab at a trestle table in
the sand on the beachfront of one of Thailand's island
resorts. The fibrous outer husks from local coconuts were
piled into a large drum, set on fire and then splashed with
water to produce an aromatic smoke. Small sand or spider
crabs were placed on wire mesh over the smoke and were
soon permeated with a delicate smoky coconut flavour.

*Set crabs on rack over wood
chips*

*Crack crab claws with a
cleaver before serving*

**4 sand crabs (each approx. 315 g/10 oz)
coconut husks (or hickory chips)**

Use a heavy cleaver to cut the husks into thin
shreds. Line the wok with several layers of
aluminium foil and put in the husks. Sprinkle on
1 to 2 tablespoons of water. Place a rack over the husks
and set the whole crabs on top. Heat until smoking, cover the
wok and smoke for about 20 minutes.

   Crack the shells with the cleaver before serving.
Delicious with icy cold beer and a chilli sauce dip.

# Smoked John Dory

SERVES 4–6

2 × 500 g (1 lb) John Dory (pomfret)
1 tablespoon dry sherry
½ teaspoon salt
2 tablespoons light soy sauce
2 teaspoons sugar
2 tablespoons finely chopped shallot (spring onion/
    scallion)
2 teaspoons grated fresh (root) ginger
2 tablespoons Chinese black tea leaves
1½ tablespoons sugar

Clean and wash the fish and wipe dry. Score deeply in several places on each side, then place in a dish. Mix the sherry, salt, soy, sugar, shallot and ginger together. Rub over the fish, then cover with a piece of plastic wrap and leave for at least 1 hour to absorb the flavours.

Line the interior of a wok with a double thickness of aluminium foil and put in the tea leaves and sugar. Set a rack over this and heat until the leaves begin to smoke.

Drain the fish and wipe with kitchen paper. Place on the rack, cover the wok and smoke over moderate heat until the fish is cooked through and is a rich golden colour (about 25 minutes), turning once or twice.

Remove from the wok and brush lightly with sesame or cooking oil to give the skin a shine. Serve with mayonnaise.

Cucumber and radish, sliced and pickled in a mixture of white vinegar, sugar and salt for about 2 hours, makes a tasty accompaniment to this dish.

*Rub flavourings over the scored John Dory*

*Line a wok with foil, add tea leaves and sugar*

# Table-top Cooking

Cooking at the table produces a distinct ambience at a dinner party. It can introduce a note of informality, or charge the occasion with a feeling of super-sophistication. It can highlight the skills of a talented amateur chef, or disguise the insecurities of the host who does not want to rely on his limited ability in the kitchen.

An elegant flambé, prepared at the table and served as the prelude to the meal, perhaps to be followed by an oven-cooked main course and a simple dessert or cheese, would make an impressive menu. Yet the host could be there at the dinner table with his guests throughout the meal, instead of finding himself with little more than a few minutes to chat and eat between excursions to the kitchen.

One-pot meals such as the Japanese *Sukiyaki* or *Tempura* can be cooked at the table, they look spectacular and taste superb and guests can participate freely in the cooking and serving. They bring to the table a casual, even intimate atmosphere which should allow conversation to flow and friendships blossom.

Few hosts want to spend time in the kitchen preparing a hot dessert. Yet on many occasions something hot, full of rich flavours and laced with liqueurs is needed to round off a menu. A table-top dessert of flambéed fruits, a sweet omelette or crêpes cooked at the table and wrapped around prepared fruit and cream fillings, are dishes that are easy on the chef and bring the dinner party to a dramatic conclusion.

There are a number of different types of portable cookers — ranging from the small electric type with a dish-shaped ring curved to accommodate a wok, to one-ring gas cookers especially made to work with a wok. These may need to be dressed up to improve their appearance for use on the table, and for this a 'skirt' of aluminium foil may be the answer. Remember too that they may become hot underneath, so place them on a thick cutting board to prevent spoiling your table top.

For even more convenience, use an electric wok for table-top cooking. It can stand directly on the table without causing heat damage, is light and is easily portable, which means that it does not need to be set up in advance but simply brought to the table when required, plugged in to a power point, and you're ready to begin.

Food to be cooked at the table should be completely prepared in advance and arranged attractively on platters. Place these near the cooker and have the required cooking utensils — the wok 'charn', a pair of tongs, a tasting spoon and a metal ladle for heating liquor for flambéeing — on a tray or cloth nearby. Plates or a serving platter should be warmed and ready as well.

Table-top meals at which guests participate in the cooking require careful organization to ensure that all have access to the uncooked food, the wok and the necessary seasonings and utensils. Depending on the number of guests, seating configuration and the size of your table, divide the uncooked ingredients evenly between several plates and place these at even intervals around the table. Have jars and bowls of seasonings, and an adequate number of the required cooking utensils grouped near the wok.

If there are more than half a dozen guests, or the table is a long one, it will be necessary to organize two separate cooking areas. This can be done without loss of the easy spirit that should go hand in hand with cook-it-yourself meals.

# Tempura

SERVES 4 AS A MAIN COURSE,
6–8 AS AN APPETIZER

The ideal way to cook *Tempura* is right there at the table, as it must come straight from the pan to be at its very best. Cover a corner of the table with a cloth, preferably plastic, and set up a portable wok or an electric wok filled with clean cooking oil. The Japanese use long thin metal chopsticks for retrieving the cooked *Tempura* from the hot oil, but wooden cooking chopsticks or tongs will do just as well.

1 green or red capsicum (bell pepper)
1 small sweet potato
1 large onion
8 shallots (spring onions/scallions)
8 French (green) beans
3 fillets sea perch or similar
   (approx. 280 g/9 oz)
3 fresh squid (approx. 125 g/4 oz)
8 medium green prawns (raw shrimp),
   (approx. 375 g/12 oz)
2 teaspoons dry sherry or
   ginger wine
pinch of salt

Batter
2 cups (8 oz) flour
½ cup (2 oz) cornflour (cornstarch)
2 medium eggs, beaten
2 cups water

Sauce
1 cup (8 fl oz) Japanese dashi stock★
½ cup (4 fl oz) light soy sauce
½ cup (4 fl oz) sweet sherry
2 tablespoons finely grated white radish
   or Japanese daikon

Trim away the seed core, stem and inner ribs of the pepper and cut it into small squares. Peel and slice the sweet potato and onion. Trim the shallots and beans but leave whole. Cut the fish into fingers and the squid into rings. De-vein the prawns and marinate with the sherry or wine, and the salt. Arrange the vegetables and seafood attractively on a large platter.

Beat the batter ingredients together. The batter should be of the consistency of lightly whipped cream. Do not overbeat, as tiny lumps are acceptable in a *Tempura* batter.

Mix the sauce ingredients together and pour into a small bowl for each guest.

When ready to serve, heat the oil to hot. Dip the ingredients into the batter and deep-fry until crisp and cooked through. Cook each different ingredient separately, and serve directly onto your guests' plates. The sauce is used as a dip.

★ *If* dashi *cannot be found at a specialist Chinese or Japanese food supplier, substitute chicken stock made with a stock cube or powder and add about ¼ cup of orange juice to give an equally tasty sauce.*

*Prepare vegetables and arrange on a platter*

*Arrange seafood attractively on a platter*

*Ingredients may be skewered then battered*

# Sizzling Sesame Beef

*Partially freeze meat to cut in paper-thin slices*

*Cut onions into wedges and separate*

**SERVES 4**

**500 g (1 lb) beef fillet (tenderloin)**
**½ teaspoon crushed garlic**
**1½ tablespoons dry sherry**
**1 tablespoon sesame oil**
**1½ tablespoons dark soy sauce (mushroom soy)**
**2 teaspoons sugar**
**2 teaspoons cornflour (cornstarch)**
**1 medium onion**
**vegetable or peanut oil**
**2 teaspoons white sesame seeds**

**Sauce**
**⅓ cup water**
**2 teaspoons dry sherry**
**1 tablespoon light soy sauce**
**1 teaspoon cornflour (cornstarch)**

Partially freeze the beef so that it is more easily cut into paper-thin slices. Place in a dish with the garlic, sherry, sesame oil, soy, sugar and cornflour. Mix well and leave for 1 to 2 hours to marinate.

Peel and halve the onion, and cut it into thin wedges. Separate each slice and set aside. Mix the sauce ingredients together in a small jug.

Heat the wok at the table. Add about 2 tablespoons of vegetable or peanut oil and put in the onions and sesame seeds. Sauté until the sesame seeds are golden, then remove.

Wipe out the wok, reheat the oil and add the beef. Sauté on high heat until just cooked (about 2½ minutes). Return the onions and sesame seeds, and pour in the sauce. Simmer briskly until the sauce thickens, then serve.

# Pepper Steaks

SERVES 6

**6 fillet (tenderloin) steaks (approx. 750 g/1½ lb)**
**60 g (2 oz) butter**
**1 tablespoon cooking oil**
**1 tablespoon flour**
**½ cup (4 fl oz) dry white wine**
**1 tablespoon brandy or cognac**
**½ cup (4 fl oz) beef stock**
**pinch of sugar**
**1 tablespoon lightly crushed black peppercorns**
**1 tablespoon canned green peppercorns, drained**
**¼ cup (2 fl oz) thickened (heavy) cream**

Trim the steaks if necessary. Assemble the ingredients at the table.

Heat the wok to moderate and add the butter and oil. Fry the steaks quickly on each side, then cook until done to taste. Remove and keep warm.

Sprinkle the flour into the wok and stir in lightly, then add the wine and bring to boil. Simmer briefly. Heat the cognac or brandy in a metal ladle, flame and pour into the wok. Add the beef stock and boil for about 3 minutes. Add the sugar and peppercorns, reduce the heat and simmer for 2 to 3 minutes. Add the cream and heat through. Serve the steaks with a generous amount of the sauce.

*Brown steaks in butter and oil, turn with 2 spoons*

*Heat cognac in metal ladle and ignite*

# Sukiyaki

SERVES 4 GENEROUSLY

*Sukiyaki* was probably the first Japanese dish to achieve recognition and acceptance in Western households, and it remains a popular dinner party feature. It is easy to prepare, fun to cook and eat, and is ideal for impromptu dinners.

**750 g (1½ lb) sirloin (striploin/porterhouse, loin) steak in one piece**
**4 squares soft beancurd (tofu)***
**2 medium onions**
**8 shallots (spring onions/scallions)**
**2 bunches watercress or spinach**
**8 dried Japanese black mushrooms, soaked**
**185 g (6 oz) shiritaki noodles or Chinese 'glass' noodles, or mung bean vermicelli**
**2–3 pieces fresh beef suet**
**4 eggs**

**Sauce**
**1 cup (8 fl oz) light soy sauce**
**1¼ cups (10 fl oz) Japanese dashi stock****
**½ cup (4 fl oz) sake (rice wine) or Japanese mirin (sweet rice wine)**
**2½ tablespoons sugar**

Trim the steak and cut into very thin slices. This can be done more easily if the meat has been partially frozen beforehand to make it firm. Arrange the meat on one or two platters.

Cut the beancurd into small cubes and place with the meat. Peel and slice the onions. Trim the shallots and leave whole. Rinse the vegetables and shake off excess water, then remove the stems. Drain the mushrooms when softened, and remove the stems; cut a cross in the top of each to decorate and to allow it to cook quicker. Drop the noodles into boiling water to soften, then drain well. Mix the sauce ingredients together in a jug.

When ready to cook, set up an electric or portable wok in the centre of the table on a cloth. Heat the wok and rub the suet over the bottom until well greased.

Hand each diner a fresh egg, to be beaten in his or her own bowl. This will be used as a dip, in conjunction with some of the prepared sauce.

Bring the meat platter and the other ingredients to the table, placing them within easy reach of the diners. Hand each person a pair of wooden chopsticks.

Fry the meat quickly, then splash on a little of the sauce to flavour. Cook portions of the remaining ingredients separately in the centre, until done to taste, adding plenty of the sauce. The diners help themselves to meat, vegetables and noodles, dipping them into the egg and sauce before eating.

* *If tofu is not available, or not appreciated, peel and slice a sweet potato and cut a capsicum (bell pepper) into squares to substitute.*

** *If dashi is unobtainable, use chicken stock powder mixed with water and add ½ cup of orange juice. Or use flaked dried bonito katsuobushi and a piece of kombu kelp boiled together to make the stock.*

Cube the tofu (bean curd)

Cut a cross on soaked mushrooms

Soak noodles in boiling water to soften

Cook portions of sukiyaki at the table

# Sweet Omelette with Strawberry Sauce

SERVES 6

Easier than a soufflé and just as tasty, sweet omelettes garnished with fruity sauces are popular in northern European countries.

**8 eggs**
**2 tablespoons milk**
**2 teaspoons cornflour (cornstarch)**
**1 tablespoon sugar**
**1 tablespoon unsalted butter**
**1 tablespoon brandy or Kirsch**

**Strawberry Sauce**
**approx. 220 g (7 oz) fresh strawberries\***
**1 cup (8 fl oz) fruity white wine**
**1 tablespoon lemon juice**
**1 tablespoon sugar**
**1 tablespoon flour**
**1½ tablespoons butter**

Prepare the sauce first. Hull the strawberries, rinse and dry, then cut into halves. Set aside. Bring the remaining sauce ingredients to the boil in a saucepan or wok and whisk briskly to incorporate the flour and sugar. When thickened, remove from the heat, add the strawberries and keep warm until needed.

Beat 5 eggs and the yolks of the remaining eggs together, adding the milk, cornflour and sugar. Beat the egg whites separately to soft peaks, then carefully fold into the batter.

Melt the butter in the wok at the table. Pour in the batter and cook, covered, over moderate heat until the omelette is lightly browned and beginning to firm up.

Fold in half and continue to cook, covered, until the inside is just firm. If the underside begins to take on too much colour, flip the folded pancake over and continue to cook gently. Make sure the heat isn't too high.

Use two egg slices (egg lifters) to carefully lift the omelette onto a serving dish. Pour on the prepared strawberry sauce. Heat the brandy or Kirsch in a metal ladle and flame. Pour over the dessert and serve at once with whipped cream.

\* *This omelette is equally delicious served with drained canned black cherries.*

*Fold whisked egg whites into yolk mixture*

*Pour into melted butter in wok*

# Cherries Jubilee

SERVES 4

**1 can 425 g (13½ oz) black cherries in syrup**
**2 tablespoons butter**
**2 tablespoons brandy or Cognac**
**1 tablespoon Kirsch**
**2 teaspoons cornflour (cornstarch)**

Drain the cherries, reserving the syrup. Melt the butter in the wok at the table and sauté the cherries for about 1 minute, then pour in the brandy or Cognac and ignite. Stir until the flames are extinguished, then add the Kirsch and boil briskly. Mix the cornflour with three-quarters of the reserved cherry syrup and pour over the cherries. Stir on moderate heat until thickened. Serve on to vanilla ice-cream.

*Sauté drained cherries in butter*

*Stir cornflour with cherry juice then add to wok*

# Tropical Fruit Flambé

SERVES 4

**4 slices canned pineapple**
**1 ripe but firm banana**
**1 passionfruit**
**2 tablespoons butter**
**2½ tablespoons soft brown sugar**
**¼ cup (2 fl oz) lime juice**
**¼ cup (2 fl oz) pineapple juice**
**1¼ tablespoons brandy**
**2 teaspoons dark rum**
**whipped cream**

Drain the pineapple. Peel the banana and cut in half lengthways, then in half again to give four pieces. Open the passionfruit and set aside.

Heat the wok and melt the butter. Add the pineapple and banana and sauté gently until the banana is beginning to soften. Sprinkle on the brown sugar, then add the juices. Heat the brandy and rum together in a metal ladle and then flame. Pour into the pan and boil briefly. Transfer the fruit to dessert dishes and top with whipped cream. Decorate with the passionfruit juice and seeds, and serve.

*Cut halved banana into four pieces*

*Heat brandy and rum in a ladle and flame*

# *Index*